ROCK-A-BYE, SAILOR!

A Comedy in Three Acts

by

PHILIP KING and FALKLAND L. CARY

SAMUEL FRENCH

LONDON

NEW YORK   TORONTO   SYDNEY   HOLLYWOOD

FOR AMATEUR PRODUCTION ENQUIRIES

UNITED KINGDOM AND WORLD
EXCLUDING NORTH AMERICA
plays@samuelfrench.co.uk
020 7255 4302/01

Each title is subject to availability from Samuel French,
depending upon country of performance.

ROCK-A-BYE, SAILOR!

Produced by Toby Rowland Ltd. at the Phoenix Theatre, London, on the 16th October 1962, with the following cast of characters:

(in the order of their appearance)

EDIE HORNETT	*Patricia Hayes*
EMMA HORNETT	*Renée Houston*
HENRY HORNETT	*Cyril Smith*
MRS FLORRIE LACK	*Margaret St Barbe West*
ALBERT TUFNELL, A.B.	*Ian Curry*
SHIRLEY TUFNELL	*Janet Butlin*
DAPHNE BLIGH	*Wanda Ventham*
CARNOUSTIE BLIGH, A.B.	*Ian MacNaughton*
ROBIN STEBBINGTON	*John Warner*

Directed by DENNIS MAIN WILSON

Setting by KEN CALDER

SYNOPSIS OF SCENES

The action of the Play passes in the living-room of the Hornetts' house in a small inland town

ACT I
An afternoon in late October

ACT II
SCENE 1 The following morning
SCENE 2 Two hours later

ACT III
Early afternoon of the same day

Time—the present

ACT I

Scene—*The living-room of the Hornetts' house in a small inland town. An afternoon in late October.*

A door down L *leads to a small hall, the front door and the stairs. A door up* R *leads to the kitchen and back door. A casement window back* C, *overlooks the back yard. The fireplace is* R. *There is a built-in cupboard up* LC, *under the stairs, and another built-in cupboard over the kitchen door. The Hornetts are a working-class family and the furnishings are ordinary in taste, but everything about the room is spotless. Down* R *is an upright chair. A small cabinet stands between the upright chair and the fireplace. Above the fireplace is a small table with a wireless receiver on it, and there is a sideboard against the wall up* R. *Two upright chairs stand* R *and* L *of the window. There is an easy chair above the fireplace and a sofa to match* LC. *A small dining-table stands* C, *with an upright chair* R *of it. There is an upright chair below the door down* L. *A small table stands in the hall* L, *and there is a kitchen cabinet in the kitchen up* R.

When the Curtain *rises, it is about 4.30 p.m.* Edie Hornett, *a thin, nondescript spinster of fortyish, is rocking an old-fashioned wooden cradle, which is on the floor down* RC, *facing up stage.*

Edie (*singing*)
> "Lula, lula, lula, lula, by-bye,
> Does you want the moon to play with?
> Or the stars to run away with . . .?"

(*She breaks down, dabs her nose with a handkerchief and sniffs brokenly. She speaks into the cradle in a choked voice*) Diddums, then? Is naughty auntie's singing keeping him awake, then? (*She smiles bravely through her tears and playfully waggles her finger*) Naughty auntie won't sing any more. (*She waggles her finger and coos, then claps her hands gently in time and recites*)

> "Jack and Jill went up the hill,
> To fetch a pail of water . . ."

(Emma Hornett *enters from the hall and stands just inside the doorway. She carries some parcels and her handbag*)

Emma (*in a voice of thunder*) Edie 'Ornett! (*She crosses to the cradle*)

(Emma *puts her foot down on the side of the cradle, which, discreetly aided by* Edie, *tips over and spills its contents on the floor. These are a blue pottie, a baby's bottle, two tins of Cow and Gate, glucose, two packets of Farex, a large bottle of cod-liver oil and a pillow.* Edie *gives a panic-stricken yelp*)

EDIE (*in a panic-stricken voice*) Emma! I didn't . . . I wasn't . . . I was just . . .

EMMA. It's 'appened! (*She moves to the hall door*) I do believe it's 'appened at last. You've taken leave of the senses you never 'ad.

(EMMA *exits to the hall and re-enters immediately, carrying a light, modern baby's cot.* EDIE *picks up and looks at the articles that have fallen from the cradle*)

EDIE (*fluttering*) I was only . . . I—I—I've done the shopping. I got all the things you said, Emma. (*She shows the various articles*) Glucose—cereal—Cow and Gate. (*She shows the baby's bottle. Sentimentally*) His little bottle and—oh, yes . . . (*She breaks off as she holds up the pottie and quickly puts it down again*) I got everything we wanted, Emma.

(EMMA *puts the cot on the sofa and moves to the cradle*)

EMMA. Pity you 'adn't stopped at that. (*She indicates the cradle*) What in the name of all that's 'orrible is this? (*She kicks the cradle*)

EDIE (*excitedly*) Oh, I bought it, Emma, myself, personal, for Shirley and Albert. It's a cradle for baby. I just 'appened to see it . . .

EMMA. "See it"? Where? The British Museum?

EDIE (*innocently*) Oh, no, Emma. The British Museum's in London. No, I got this at the second-hand shop at the corner of the High Street. (*She pats the cradle*) It's antique, Emma.

EMMA (*crossing to the sideboard*) I'm not blind. (*She puts her parcels and handbag on the sideboard*)

EDIE. The man at the shop said it belonged to the Mary Queen of Scots.

EMMA (*crossing to the sofa*) Then the sooner it goes back to 'er, the better. (*She picks up the cot and moves* C) This is more like it.

EDIE. Oh, Emma, you've got one, too.

EMMA. And this is the one they'll 'ave. (*She puts the cot on the sofa*)

EDIE. Well, fancy! Still, they do say great minds think alike.

EMMA (*grimly*) I doubt if your great mind's thinking what mine is right now. (*She indicates the articles out of the cradle*) Get this lot cleared away—(*she crosses to the fireplace*) and that thing—(*she points to the cradle*) out of sight. (*She looks at the clock*) Shirley and that 'usband of 'ers'll be here soon, and we don't want the place looking like a baby farm *before* they arrive.

EDIE (*dragging the cradle down* R) Oo! I can't wait to see the baby, can you, Emma?

EMMA (*removing her hat; grimly*) I've 'ad to wait three weeks—I can manage a bit longer. (*She puts her hat on the sideboard*)

EDIE (*crossing to* C) Shirley must be so 'appy. (*She sniffs brokenly*) I wonder who he takes after? (*She picks up the articles that fell from the cradle*)

EMMA. Eh?

EDIE. I mean—Shirley or Albert?

EMMA (*removing her coat*) If he's any sense he'll take after our side of the family. One Albert Tufnell in this world's quite enough.

EDIE. Do you think *he'll* grow up to be a sailor like his dad?

EMMA. No, he won't.

EDIE. But how do you know?

EMMA. I've *said* so, haven't I? (*She moves and stands over Edie*) And I'll thank you not to put your spoke in. Understand?

EDIE. Yes, Emma.

EMMA. Right! Then let's get the tea laid. (*She moves to the sideboard*) Their train's due in a quarter of an hour and there'll be Henry dribbling in any minute now.

(EDIE *moves to the kitchen door*)

(*She takes a parcel from the sideboard and hands it to Edie*) Here, take these into the back kitchen. They're sausage rolls; I thought they might help out with the boiled 'am. (*She opens the kitchen door*)

EDIE. Yes, Emma. Though I expect baby'll prefer sausage rolls.

(EDIE *exits to the kitchen and is heard clattering china.* EMMA *glares after Edie for a moment, then takes a white cloth from the sideboard drawer and spreads it on the table*)

EMMA (*calling loudly*) And, Edie——

EDIE (*off*) Yes?

EMMA. —when they *do* get here and while they *are* here, I'll thank you not to go making a fool of yourself over the baby, understand? Don't let me catch you slobbering over it, and tellin' it all about your "Great Sorrow". It'll 'ave plenty of "great sorrows" of its own soon enough, if I'm any judge. The way they go pampering children these days makes me sick, fillin' 'em up with orange juice and the Lord knows what from the first second they're born—rushin' 'em off to clinics to be weighed every five minutes, and treatin' 'em as if they were made of cut glass instead of flesh and blood. (*Louder still*) That baby'll get no pampering in this 'ouse. We'll give it the attention it's due and no more. And we don't want no "Jack and Jills went up the hills" from *you*, Edie 'Ornett.

(HENRY HORNETT, *Emma's husband, enters from the hall and crosses to the fireplace. He is a smallish man of fifty, with a drooping moustache. He wears a shapeless, but clean blue suit*)

(*She turns at once, points an accusing finger at Henry and speaks almost in the same breath*) And that goes for you, too.

HENRY (*removing his tie; phlegmatically*) What does?

EMMA. I was just trying to drill it into this sister of yours that when Shirley and that 'usband of 'ers and the baby arrive—(*in a firmer voice*) which they will very soon now, so——

(HENRY *starts to remove his collar*)

—I'll thank you to leave that collar where it is. (*She moves to the sofa*

and thumps the cushions) There's no call for you to show yourself to
your grandchild for the first time stark naked.

(HENRY *fixes his collar and re-knots his tie*)

I was just telling Edie, I'm not going to have it thrown in my face
that the child was spoilt under my roof. You got that clear, 'Enry?
    HENRY. If anybody interferes with the kid in this 'ouse, it won't
be me.
    EMMA (*with a step towards Henry; sharply*) What are you throwin'
out?
    HENRY. I'm just statin' a fact. I've got enough youngsters of my
own to worry about, without interfering with anybody else's.
    EMMA. *What?*
    HENRY. Rosie's just 'ad another litter—this mornin'. Eight of
'em this time.
    EMMA (*contemptuously*) Ferrets!
    HENRY. *'Course!* What d'you expect a ferret to give birth to—
goldfish?

(EDIE *enters from the kitchen carrying a tray of tea things which she
puts on the table*)

(*He moves to* R *of the table*) Edie, did you feed the ferrets at dinner-
time same as I told you?
    EDIE. Ooh! No, Henry, I forgot. I'm sorry.
    HENRY (*in great alarm*) My God! Eight youngsters and nothing
to eat since mornin'! She'll 'ave ate the lot by now.

(HENRY *exits quickly to the kitchen.* EMMA *crosses to the kitchen door*)

EMMA (*calling after Henry*) I'll give you five minutes, 'Enry 'Ornett
and no more. We don't want you breathin' ferrets all over Shirley's
baby. (*Louder*) And let me catch you taking it out to see them things
and . . . (*She turns*) I'd divorce that man tomorrow if they'd let me
cite them ferrets as co-respondents.

(EDIE *crosses to the cradle*)

(*Sharply*) And I thought I told you to get rid of that?
    EDIE. Shall I put it in Shirley and Albert's bedroom—or hadn't
we better wait and let them decide which they'd like—yours or
mine?
    EMMA. I 'ave decided—they'll like mine.
    EDIE (*crossing to the cot on the sofa*) 'Course, this *is* very nice—in
a way—if you like this sort of thing, that is.
    MRS LACK (*off up* L; *calling*) Yoo-hoo! Are you there, Emma?
    EMMA (*growling*) Oh, my Lord!
    EDIE. It's Mrs Lack, Emma.

(MRS FLORRIE LACK *enters* L, *outside the window, and crosses to the
back door. She is much the same age as Emma. She takes life easily, and
other folks' troubles with considerable pleasure*)

EMMA. 'Course it's Mrs Lack. It's always Mrs Lack. No-one would think that woman 'ad a 'ome of 'er own. (*She moves to the fireplace*)

(MRS LACK *enters from the kitchen*)

MRS LACK (*as she enters*) Are you there, Emma? Oh, there you are. It's only me.

EMMA (*muttering*) An' you're too many.

MRS LACK. I just thought I'd pop in and see if Shirley and Albert . . . (*She sees Edie bending over the cot. With great fuss and in a sentimental voice*) Oh, they 'ave arrived, and there's the baby, bless it. (*As she crosses towards the cot*) Oh, Emma, isn't it beautiful and the spitten image of you. (*By this time she has reached the cot and now looks into it*) Oh! (*Her hand goes into the cot and comes out holding a large golliwog. She looks embarrassedly towards Emma*) Oh, I say!

(EMMA *glares at Mrs Lack*)

(*She moves* C) Aren't I a silly?

EMMA (*moving to* R *of Mrs Lack*) Yes, you are, *aren't* you?

MRS LACK. It was seeing the cot—naturally I thought . . . Still, I'm sure it *will* look like you. Did they send the cot on in advance?

EMMA (*shortly*) No, they did not. If you must know, *I've* bought it for Shirley—as a surprise.

MRS LACK. Oh, Emma, that's kind of you. (*She turns to Edie*) Isn't that kind of 'er, Edie?

EDIE (*moving to* L *of Mrs Lack*) Very, but, you see, I've been kind, too. (*She points to the cradle*) I've bought that.

MRS LACK (*golliwog in hand; crossing to the cradle*) My God! What's that—a coffin?

(EDIE *turns away, gives a little howl of misery, takes out her handkerchief and sobs into it*)

Oh, I'm sorry if I've said something I shouldn't, but just for the moment, it looked like . . . It's very nice, Edie, very nice indeed —if you like that sort of thing, that is. (*She moves to* R *of Emma*) Eh, Emma?

(EDIE *sniffs*)

EMMA. Very nice if you want the child to wake up every mornin' with one of them slipped discs. (*To Edie*) Put it behind there—(*she points up* L) out of sight.

(EDIE *crosses to the cradle, picks it up and puts it on the floor in the corner up* L)

Shirley can see it when she comes, and we'll explain that you meant well. (*She takes the golliwog from Mrs Lack*) And if you can bear to part with this, Florrie . . . (*She makes a great show of dusting the golliwog with her hands, rather suggesting "contamination" from Mrs Lack*) You'll excuse us if we get on, won't you? (*She puts the golliwog in the cot*) We don't seem to be so lucky as some folk—with all the time in the world on their 'ands. Edie!

(EDIE *moves to the cot. She and* EMMA *move it against the wall above the hall door*)

MRS LACK (*blithely*) Oh, that's all right, Emma. (*She moves to the fireplace*)

(EMMA *is about to retort, but* MRS LACK *goes on*)

And, havin' the christening tomorrow, I suppose it's thrown you more out of gear than ever.

EMMA (*almost choking with rage; in a suppressed voice*) Edie, don't just stand there copying Florrie—doin' nothing; we've got to get this table laid.

EDIE (*moving above the table; flurried*) Yes, Emma. I was just goin' to. (*She picks up a knife and fork and poises them ready to put on the table*) Where's baby goin' to sit?

EMMA (*moving to L of the table; with great sarcasm*) Oh, it'll sit in my place, naturally.

(EDIE, *holding the knife and fork, moves to the right end of the table*)

We'll get it to pour the tea for a change. (*Irritably*) It won't sit anywhere, *and* it won't want those. (*She moves above the table to L of Edie, snatches the knife and fork from her and slams them down on to the table*) What d'you think Shirley's given birth to—an infant prodigal? (*Curtly*) Bread and butter.

(EDIE *exits to the kitchen*)

MRS LACK (*sitting in the easy chair*) Poor Edie, she 'asn't much idea, 'as she?

EMMA. She 'asn't anything to 'ave an idea with.

MRS LACK. But—you haven't seen the baby yourself, yet, 'ave you?

EMMA (*shortly*) I 'ave not.

MRS LACK. Funny! I should 'ave thought Shirley would 'ave wanted you there when it was born.

EMMA (*moving to R of the table; shortly*) So should I—but I wasn't asked. Think of it! That child born three weeks ago. Only a few miles away and it 'asn't seen me, its own grandmother, yet.

MRS LACK. But I thought you went over to Portsmouth the day it was born?

EMMA. I did go. I'm 'uman, aren't I?

MRS LACK. We all are, come to that. 'Course, some are more 'uman than others.

EMMA. Well, I'm ever so 'uman. I was determined that child should 'ave its rights. "If the mountain can't come to its grandmother," I said, "its grandmother will go to the mountain."

MRS LACK. Fancy!

EMMA. So I went over to Portsmouth the day the baby was expected—brand new, the hospital was.

MRS LACK. Really?

EMMA. "Royalty" was coming down to open it officially that very afternoon.

MRS LACK (*almost gushing*) Royalty? Ooh—that was nice, wasn't it?

EMMA. It wasn't nice. In fact it was far *from* nice. It was only ten o'clock in the morning when I arrived, and the "opening" wasn't until two, but was I allowed in to see my own daughter? I was not. Nothing short of a title as long as my arm would 'ave got me through the door—not till the place was opened official. I just came away.

MRS LACK. Never mind, Emma. You're seeing the child today.

EMMA. And no thanks to Mr Albert Tufnell for that. Didn't even want that child to be christened in Shirley's own church—where she was christened 'erself. (*She moves to the kitchen door and calls*) Edie, are you buttering that bread or baking it? (*She moves to R of the table*) But I wrote to Shirley pretty straight. "Shirley," I said, "do you want to break your mother's heart *altogether?* If your child can't come to your old 'ome to be christened, it needn't come at all," I said. "And you can tell that 'usband of yours so with my compliments."

MRS LACK. She'll 'ave to learn to stand up to him more, won't she?

EMMA (*crossing to the fireplace*) How can she? How can any woman once a man 'as 'er in his clutches? From the day he 'ands over 'is first pay-packet she's 'ad it. The fact that he's the one that's bringing the money into the 'ouse—it goes to 'is 'ead like wine, and 'e starts 'is "Lord and mastering" and before she knows where she is—'e's treating 'er like a doormat for 'im to wipe 'is feet on.

(HENRY *enters from the kitchen and moves to the cabinet down* R)

(*To Henry; immediately*) And what are you up to *now?*

HENRY. I'm not up to nothing.

EMMA. Then it's time you were, and for a start you can go and get yourself washed.

(HENRY *moves to the kitchen door*)

(*Quickly*) And not in there! Edie's cuttin' bread and butter and we don't want it tasting of soapsuds. You can use the bathroom.

(HENRY *crosses to* C)

(*She follows to* R *of Henry*) And remember it *is* a bathroom, not a public swimming bath.

(HENRY *crosses towards the hall door*)

(*She turns to Mrs Lack*) Now—where was I?

MRS LACK. Being a doormat for him to wipe his feet on.

Emma. Oh, yes.

(Henry *pauses at the cot and takes out the golliwog*)

Henry (*holding up the golliwog and speaking to Emma; placidly*)
Hello! You bin unfaithful?

(Henry *replaces the golliwog in the cot and exits to the hall*) ·

Emma (*moving to the sideboard*) You see what I mean, Florrie?

(Edie *enters from the kitchen, carrying a plate of bread and butter*)

Edie (*as she enters*) How many slices of bread and butter shall I
cut, Emma? (*She puts the plate on the table*)
Emma (*to Mrs Lack*) Now I've got to turn myself into a chartered
accountant and start reckoning . . . (*To Edie. Irritably*) Cut a couple
of platefuls and if there isn't enough you can cut some more later.
Are you nearly ready now for when they come?
Edie (*fluttering*) Oo! I think so, Emma. (*She straightens her dress*)
I was going to change into my new flowered silk, but p'raps I'd
better not. I mean—well, you know what I mean—baby won't be
'ouse-trained, yet.
Mrs Lack. Have they decided what they're going to call it?
Emma (*moving to the fireplace*) I haven't decided final yet.
Mrs Lack (*sentimentally*) If I had a boy I should call him
"Trevor".
Emma (*derisively*) *Would* you? Then it's lucky for the poor thing
you won't be 'aving it, isn't it?
Mrs Lack (*unheeding*) After Trevor Howard. He's my favourite
film star. And so 'andsome.
Edie (*ecstatically*) Ooo! Isn't he wonderful, Mrs Lack? Wonderful!
But I can't bear to watch him.
Mrs Lack. Why ever not?
Edie (*crossing below the table to* L; *with a sniff*) He brings back
memories; reminds me too much of . . . (*She weeps into her apron*)
Mrs Lack (*to Emma*) *Not* 'er "great sorrow" again?

(Edie *moves to the window*)

Emma (*to Edie*) If I remember rightly, the man who left you 'igh
and dry at the altar rails—twenty years ago—was bald as a coot,
and as blind as a bat and knee-high to a grasshopper, an' if this
"Trevor-whoever-he-is" is anything like '*im,* I don't admire your
taste, Florrie.
Mrs Lack (*protesting*) Oh, but my Trevor isn't a bit like that.
'E's . . .
Edie (*looking out of the window; excitedly*) Emma! They're here!

(Mrs Lack *rises. She and* Emma *hurry to the window.* Edie *kneels
on the chair* R *of the window and leans out.* Emma *is behind Edie.* Mrs
Lack *is* R *of Emma. They peer out of the window to* L)

There's a taxi just pulled up at the front gate.

EMMA (*with a snort*) Trust Albert Tufnell to 'ave a taxi. Money's no object where sailors are concerned.

MRS LACK. Yes, there they are. She looks ever so peaky—Shirley—doesn't she? It's taken it out of 'er, 'asn't it—'avin' the baby?

EMMA (*moving to L of the table; sententiously*) The woman always pays.

EDIE (*calling and waving out of the window*) Yoo-hoo!

EMMA (*suddenly turning on Edie*) And, Edie, we don't want you 'anging out of the window like a Union Jack. (*She drags Edie from the window*) Go and give 'Enry a call.

EDIE (*darting to the hall door*) Yes, Emma.

EMMA. And tell him . . .

EDIE. Yes, Emma.

(EDIE *exits to the hall*)

(*Off; calling excitedly*) 'Enry! 'Enry! They're here.

(EDIE *re-enters from the hall*)

Shirley and Albert and Baby Bunting.

(EDIE *exits to the hall*)

(*Off; calling*) They're here!

EMMA (*snorting*) Baby Bunting!

EDIE (*off; calling*) 'Urry down, 'Enry!

(EDIE *re-enters from the hall*)

They've come in a taxi 'cos money's no object. (*She stands in the doorway and calls*) Hurry, Henry!

EMMA (*to Mrs Lack; fuming*) I mean to say . . .

EDIE (*moving to L of Emma; breathlessly*) Shall I open the front door, Emma?

EMMA. I don't see how they're goin' to get through it else.

(*The front-door bell rings*)

EDIE (*wildly*) Oo! They're here.

(EMMA *moves LC*)

They've beaten me to it!

(EDIE *exits to the hall*)

(*Off; calling*) Comin', Shirley love! Comin'.

EMMA (*shouting to Edie*) Edie, stop makin' a fool of yourself. We don't want that Albert Tufnell thinkin' he's as welcome as the flowers in May, 'cos he *isn't*. (*To Mrs Lack*) And now, Florrie, if you *don't* mind . . . (*She indicates the back door with her thumb*)

MRS LACK (*moving down R*) Oh, but, Emma, I can't go, not until I've seen the baby.

(EMMA *crosses to* RC.

 EDIE *enters from the hall, carrying a carry-cot*)

EDIE (*delirious*) Emma, he's here! I've got him. Oh, isn't he wonderful! (*She quickly puts the carry-cot on the floor* C *and kneels beside it*) Bless him, then; bless him!

EMMA (*alarmed*) Edie 'Ornett! Come away from that child. You're not safe.

 (EDIE *heeds not. She rocks the carry-cot*)

EDIE (*crooning excitedly*)
    "Lula, lula, lula, lula, by-bye . . ."

 (EMMA *marches to* EDIE, *takes her by the shoulders and drags her clear of the carry-cot*)

EMMA (*furiously*) That's right! Give the poor little mite a splitting 'eadache the minute he gets here, and have 'im beggin' for aspirin.

EDIE. Aspirin? (*She rushes to the carry-cot and gazes into it. Fervently*) I've just bought a new bottle of fifty; he can have the lot if he wants 'em, bless him. (*Rapturously*) Oh, Emma, isn't he beautiful?

 (EMMA *bends over the carry-cot.* MRS LACK *moves to* R *of it*)

MRS LACK (*gazing into the carry-cot*) Isn't he just! Beautiful!

EMMA (*in spite of herself*) Well, I must say . . .

MRS LACK. 'Course you must; you couldn't do otherwise. 'E's 'eaven—sheer 'eaven. (*Solemnly and slowly*) Emma, you're to be congratulated.

EMMA (*with a catch in her voice*) Thank you, Florrie. (*She dives into her pocket for her handkerchief and dissolves into tears*)

EDIE (*bewildered*) But, Mrs Lack, he's *Shirley's* baby, not . . .

MRS LACK (*irritably*) 'Old your noise, Edie!

 (*They all three gaze into the carry-cot,* EMMA *still sniffing sentimentally. All three sniff, first* EMMA, *then* EDIE, *then* MRS LACK)

(*Ostentatiously carried away*) I 'aven't seen nothing so lovely, not since my Evadne was first put into my arms.

EMMA (*at once her old self*) If I call to mind, your Evadne was born smothered in nettle-rash. And for goodness' sake keep your voice down. Can't you see the child's asleep?

EDIE (*gazing into the carry-cot*) He's fast asleep, the lamb.

EMMA (*kneeling beside the carry-cot*) That's right, my love, sleep tight, 'cos God knows you've plenty of sleepless times a'ead.

 (EDIE, *unable to get close to the carry-cot, peers over Emma's shoulder*)

EDIE (*singing desperately*)
    "Rock-a-bye baby,
    On the tree-top . . ."

EMMA (*sharply*) Shut up! (*Into the carry-cot*) There! There! My angel!

(ALBERT TUFNELL, A.B., *appears at the open window. He is aged twenty-four, good-looking, self-possessed, but not aggressively so. He is in his A.B. uniform and carries a large teddy bear under his arm*)

ALBERT (*fairly loudly*) Somebody talking about me?
EMMA (*at once; loudly and before she has time to get to her feet and see who it is*) Who's that kicking up all that din? (*She rises, turns and sees Albert*) Oh, it's *you*, is it?
ALBERT (*guardedly*) 'S right, Ma. It's me.
EMMA. Can't you see there's a child asleep in here?
ALBERT (*laconically*) Mine.
EMMA (*sharply*) *And* my daughter's!
ALBERT. Yeah—it was a joint effort.
EMMA (*moving to R of the window*) And what are you standing out there for? Where's Shirley?
ALBERT. On the front-door step.
EMMA. On the . . . What's she doing there?
ALBERT (*patiently*) The door's locked, and not 'aving a key——
EDIE. Ooh!
ALBERT. —we can't get in.
EMMA (*turning furiously on Edie*) Edie 'Ornett . . .
EDIE (*moving to L of the table*) I'm sorry, Emma, but you see—Shirley handed me the cot, and not wantin' baby to be in a draught I—I shut the door. I meant to go back and open it, but . . . I'm sorry, Albert.
ALBERT (*smiling*) That's O.K., Aunt Edie, don't you worry.
EMMA (*to Albert*) If you don't mind, *I'll* tell 'er whether she's to worry or not.
ALBERT (*rather irritably*) I wish you'd tell her to open the front door—or open it yourself. It's bloody cold out here.

(EDIE, *horrified, exits to the hall*)

EMMA. That's right! Swear in front of your own son.
MRS LACK (*looking into the carry-cot*) It's all right—I don't think baby 'eard, Emma.
ALBERT (*noticing Mrs Lack for the first time; muttering*) Oh, my God! Not you as well!

(ALBERT *exits outside the window to L*)

MRS LACK (*furiously*) Well, of course—if I'm not wanted . . . (*She makes pretence of going to the back door*)
EMMA (*bringing Mrs Lack down RC; on the defensive*) And who says you're not wanted?
MRS LACK. Didn't you hear what he—(*she nods towards the window*) said? "My God! Not you as well!" That's what he said. (*Puzzled*) Not me as well as *who*? (*She looks at Emma and realizes*) Oh!
EMMA. Oh—he did—did he? (*She is about to explode*)
EDIE (*off L*) Leave it there, Shirley love. I'll run it up to your room. You go and see your mother.

(SHIRLEY TUFNELL *enters from the hall. She is about twenty-three years of age. She is a pleasant-natured girl but occasionally one sees "Emma" coming out in her*)

SHIRLEY (*genuinely*) Mum! (*She runs to Emma*)
EMMA (*also genuinely*) Shirley! It's lovely to 'ave you 'ome.

(*They embrace*)

My little girl.
SHIRLEY. Hello, Mrs Lack.
EMMA (*holding Shirley at arm's length*) Let me look at you. (*Critically*) You're thinner.
SHIRLEY (*with a little laugh*) Well—I should hope so. (*She kneels* L *of the carry-cot*) Don't forget I gave birth to a ten-pound baby only three weeks ago. I reckon any girl would look a *bit* different after that.
EMMA (*moving up* R *of Shirley and bending over her*) You're not 'iding anything from me, are you? That 'usband of yours, 'e's treating you right?
SHIRLEY. 'Course he is, Mum; he's wonderful. (*Anxiously*) And, Mum, you will be—nice to Albert, won't you, while we're here? I know you two don't exactly hit it off together, but . . .
EMMA (*on the defensive*) And whose fault is that?
SHIRLEY (*rising*) Look, don't let's go into that. Just try, Mum, try ever so hard. (*In her anxiety she does not realize what she is saying*) If you knew how I had to plead and plead to get him to . . . (*She pulls up quickly, kneels at the carry-cot and clumsily tries to change the subject*) What do you think of the baby, Mrs Lack?
EMMA. You 'ad to what, did you say?

(*The following seven speeches are said more or less simultaneously*)

MRS LACK. We were just saying what a perfect picture he looks, weren't we, Emma? Lovely little . . .
EMMA (*not to be side-tracked; to Shirley; firmly*) You 'ad to plead and plead to get him to *what?*
SHIRLEY (*to Emma; with assumed vagueness*) What? (*To Mrs Lack. Quickly*) I won't take him out of his cot—not while he's asleep.
MRS LACK. Of course not, bless him.
EMMA. What did you say you had to do?
SHIRLEY (*obviously talking for the sake of it*) He was awake all the time in the train; didn't go off till we got in the taxi at this end— I daren't risk waking him now.
MRS LACK. No—I shouldn't if I were you.
EMMA. Shirley, I asked you what you had to plead and plead with Albert Tufnell about?
SHIRLEY (*with assumed brightness*) Oh, that! It was nothing, Mum, nothing at all. Forget it.
MRS LACK (*doing her best*) Well, as I *always* say, let sleeping dogs lie.

EMMA (*rounding on Mrs Lack*) Florrie Lack, in all the twenty years I've known you, you've never *mentioned* sleeping dogs. So I'll thank you to keep out of this. Now then, Shirley, let's 'ave it. What had you to plead and plead about?
SHIRLEY (*with troubled exasperation*) Oh, Mum . . .
EMMA. Don't keep "Oh, Mum-ing" me. I want to know.

(HENRY *and* ALBERT *enter from the hall*)

HENRY (*as they enter*) My, but you're looking well, lad.
ALBERT (*cheerfully*) I'm *feeling* marvellous, Pop.
HENRY. Fancy! And *married* an' all.

(SHIRLEY *rises thankfully, rushes to Henry and flings herself into his arms*)

SHIRLEY. Hello, Dad!
HENRY. Hello, love. (*He kisses Shirley*) And how are *you* lookin'? (*He holds her at arm's length*) Well, well! Married life doesn't seem to 'ave done you any 'arm.
EMMA. *Doesn't* it!
SHIRLEY (*laughing*) Not a bit.
HENRY. No. (*Reflectively*) 'Course, women've got more stamina than men. (*To Albert*) Here—young man—manners—what about ma?
ALBERT (*crossing to* L *of Emma; awkwardly*) How are you keeping, Ma—er—Mum?

(SHIRLEY *and* HENRY *move down* L)

EMMA. I don't have time to stop and think 'ow *I'm* keeping. (*She looks Albert up and down*) But *you* look fit enough, and I only wish I could say the same for Shirley, in spite of what her father says.
SHIRLEY. I'm all right, Mum.
HENRY. 'Course she is. (*He crosses and stands above the carry-cot*) Now, where's this young grandson of mine?

(ALBERT *moves to* L *of Henry.* SHIRLEY *moves to* L *of Albert*)

(*He speaks into the carry-cot*) Now, young feller-me-lad! What 'ave you got to say for yourself?
EMMA. Nothing. And neither 'ave *you*. He doesn't want you waking him up to play *Twenty Questions*. (*She stands* R *of the carry-cot*) And keep your voice down, if you must talk at all.
MRS LACK. What do you think of your grandson, Mr 'Ornett?
HENRY (*jokingly*) There doesn't seem to be much of 'im, Albert.
ALBERT (*grinning*) Don't blame me. I did *my* best
SHIRLEY. Albert!
HENRY. Why, dammit, my ferrets can do better than this.
ALBERT (*grinning*) So they should. They get more practice. (*He gives Henry a little dig in the ribs, and chuckles*)

B

(HENRY *chuckles.* ALBERT *puts his cap on Henry's head.* HENRY *crosses to* R, *puts Albert's cap on the cabinet* R *then sits in the easy chair*)

EMMA (*sharply*) And that's quite enough of that "Captain's Cabin" talk.

(SHIRLEY *removes her coat and puts it over the left end of the sofa.* ALBERT *sits on the sofa at the right end of it*)

When Edie condescends to show 'erself, we'll be seeing about tea, so—(*pointedly*) if you don't mind, Florrie . . .

(SHIRLEY *sits* L *of Albert on the sofa*)

MRS LACK (*blandly*) No, I don't mind. (*She crosses below Emma to* L *of the table*)

EMMA. Don't think I'm 'inting, but you 'ave got a 'ome of your own, 'aven't you?

MRS LACK. Yes, and Evadne'll be wondering where I've got to.

EMMA (*with meaning*) I expect she's got a rough idea.

SHIRLEY. How is Evadne, Mrs Lack?

MRS LACK. She's in the pink, bless 'er. I'd love her to see the baby. She's only a child, but ever so interested. Would it be all right if I brought her in some time?

SHIRLEY. Of course.

MRS LACK. Lovely! (*She crosses to* L *of Emma*)

EMMA. No!

MRS LACK. What?

EMMA. Well, you can't be too careful, can you, but I've always suspected that your Evadne's one of them germ-carriers.

MRS LACK (*fuming*) Well, I don't know! I've *never* heard . . .

EMMA (*almost propelling Mrs Lack towards the kitchen door*) Now I'm not blaming you—*or* Evadne. What you *can* do is bring Evadne into the yard some time, and we'll show her Shirley's baby through the window.

MRS LACK (*in high dudgeon*) Thank you *very* much.

EMMA (*ignoring the high dudgeon*) Not at all; it'll be a pleasure.

(MRS LACK *glares at Emma, but unable to find words, gives a big indignant "Oh", goes into the kitchen, and exits outside the window to* L)

(*She closes the door and moves* RC) Well, that's *one* less. I can't stand hordes of people round me, not these days. I'm getting past it.

ALBERT (*rising and moving to* L *of the table*) Look, Ma, if you'd rather Shirley and me went down to the *Rose and Crown*, you've only got to say so.

(SHIRLEY *rises and stands* R *of the sofa*)

EMMA. I dunno, 'Enry 'Ornett; some husbands seem to 'ave far more money to throw about than you ever 'ad. I don't remember you ever taking me to no *Rose and Crowns*. (*To Albert*) You'll suit yourself, of course—(*she moves to the carry-cot*) but 'eaven knows it's little enough I see of my own daughter these days—to say nothing of my grandchild three weeks old, that I 'aven't been allowed to see at all yet.

SHIRLEY (*sitting on the sofa, at the right end of it*) Of course we're staying here, Mum. Albert knows very well we can't afford the *Rose and Crown*. (*To Albert*) And talking of money—where's my change?

ALBERT (*moving to R of the sofa*) Change?

SHIRLEY. I gave you a ten-shilling note to pay the taxi. There must have been some change.

ALBERT (*feeling in his pocket*) Oh—yes.

EMMA. I'm glad to see that at least you let your wife 'old the purse-strings. (*She moves up RC*)

HENRY (*rising*) And why not? You 'old mine. (*He crosses to Albert*) I should've warned you, lad, before you got married. Never 'and your pay packet over to the wife; biggest mistake you can make; makes 'em think they're the lord and master and before you know where you are they're treatin' you like a doormat for them to wipe their feet on.

(EMMA *moves to* R *of Henry.* HENRY, *embarrassed, crosses to the easy chair, sits, takes out his pipe and lights it*)

ALBERT (*handing some coins to Shirley*) Two and six the taxi and a shilling tip.

(SHIRLEY *puts the coins in her handbag*)

EMMA (*moving* C) Three and six for a taxi. I should've thought you could've managed that short distance on a bus.

ALBERT. So should I.

EMMA (*surprised*) What?

ALBERT (*to Shirley*) What did I say? (*To Emma. Smiling*) It was Shirl who wanted the taxi, not me.

EMMA (*deflated*) Oh. Oh—well—er . . . (*Suddenly in form again*) Where's Edie, and what's she think she's doing? 'Ave you got un-packed, Shirley? You 'aven't, have you? I've got to see about tea. (*She moves to the kitchen door and turns*) And 'Enry!

(SHIRLEY *rises*)

HENRY. Yes, Emma?

EMMA. That pipe; just you go steady with it, 'cos 'eaven help you if I come back and find that child gassed. Off with you, Shirley.

(EMMA *exits to the kitchen*)

SHIRLEY. I'll just see if baby's comfy.

ALBERT (*with a faint smile*) I hope he is. (*He picks up the carry-cot and puts it on the sofa*) There we are, then.

SHIRLEY (*looking into the carry-cot*) He's all right.

ALBERT (*moving* C) Ma seems to be "on form", doesn't she?

SHIRLEY (*moving to* L *of Albert*) She'll be all right so long as nobody upsets her.

HENRY. 'Ope springs eternal . . .

ALBERT (*to Shirley*) When you say "nobody" you mean me, don't you?

SHIRLEY. All I ask is that you don't go out of your *way* to upset her.

HENRY. There's no need.

SHIRLEY (*crossing to Henry*) And that goes for you, too, Dad— (*she kisses the top of his head*) at least while *we're* here. (*She crosses towards the hall door*) I must go upstairs.

ALBERT (*stopping Shirley*) Just a minute, Shirl, but—(*he turns to Henry*) I know it's only for the week-end, but don't you think it would be better if we *did* stay at the *Rose and Crown?*

HENRY (*heartily*) 'Course it would.

ALBERT (*brightening*) Well, then . . .

HENRY. But Gawd 'elp you if you tried it on.

ALBERT (*flatly*) Oh!

HENRY. You'd 'ave Emma down there after you like a nuclear bomb and she'd explode right in the residents' lounge.

ALBERT. But, Pop, surely, if ma knows the others are staying at the *Rose and Crown*, too . . . ?

HENRY (*rising*) Others? What others?

ALBERT. Why—Daphne and Carnoustie.

HENRY (*blinking*) Daphne and . . . ?

ALBERT (*laughing*) Now, come on, Pop—pull yourself together— you're not as old as all that. *Ma's niece*—Daphne—she married my best man—Carnoustie.

HENRY (*smiling*) I'll kick your behind for you in a minute, young man. *And* in front of your own son. 'Course I remember 'em, dammit, but—what are they doing over here, *and* staying at the *Rose and Crown?*

ALBERT (*somewhat puzzled*) Why, they're coming over for the christening, didn't ma tell you?

(SHIRLEY, *looking troubled, sits on the sofa*)

HENRY. No, she didn't—and for a damn good reason.

ALBERT. What reason?

HENRY. She doesn't know. (*He sits in the easy chair*)

ALBERT. What? But—(*he crosses to* R *of the sofa*) Shirl, you told her in your last letter . . . (*He sees Shirley's look*) You did tell her, didn't you?

SHIRLEY (*guiltily*) No, Albert.

ALBERT (*baffled*) But—but . . . (*With some irritation*) Why the hell didn't you?

SHIRLEY (*desperately*) Well, I—I thought perhaps it was best not to. Mum didn't get on well with either of them at our wedding, remember?

ALBERT (*moving* RC) At our wedding your ma didn't even get on with herself. But what's that got to do with . . . ?

SHIRLEY (*still desperately*) Well, I thought if she knew they were coming here today, she'd think I'd expect her to ask them here, and I knew that if I did ask them they'd refuse, and that would get mum's back up, and . . .

(ALBERT *sits on the right arm of the sofa*)

HENRY (*rising and moving* C) 'Ere, 'alf a minute! I'm gettin' dizzy.

ALBERT. That makes two of us.

HENRY. What you're trying to say is—that Daphne and her husband are coming for the christening and your mother doesn't know.

ALBERT. That's about it, Pop.

HENRY. And, my God, it's enough. She'll play 'ell.

SHIRLEY (*desperately*) But if they don't come here—to the house . . .

HENRY. For God's sake, Shirley, surely you know your mother well enough by now? If they *don't* come she'll play 'ell because they *'aven't*, and if they *do* come she'll play 'ell because they *'ave*. Not that it matters very much, 'cos if she'd nothing to play 'ell about, she'd play 'ell about that, too.

ALBERT. You know Carnoustie and Daphne have got a baby, too, don't you, Pop—a daughter?

HENRY (*sitting in the easy chair*) Yes, I *do* know that; so does Emma, thank God. (*With a start*) Are they bringing it with 'em?

ALBERT. Blimey! I hope not.

HENRY. She'll play 'ell if they do.

(EDIE *enters from the hall, having changed her dress.* ALBERT *whistles*)

EDIE (*as she enters; anxiously*) 'Enry, Emma hasn't been wanting me, has she?

HENRY. She's in the kitchen, sobbing 'er 'eart out for you.

EDIE. I just thought, while I was upstairs, I'd change into my new flowered silk.

HENRY. Very thoughtful, Edie. Emma'll appreciate that.

SHIRLEY. It's lovely, Aunt Edie; isn't it, Albert?

(ALBERT *rises, crosses to Edie, picks her up and swings her round to* L *of Henry*)

ALBERT. Smashin'! I've always said it was you I ought to 'ave married, Aunt Edie.

EDIE (*writhing with delight and coyness*) Oh, Albert, aren't you awful!

HENRY. There's nothin' to stop you takin' 'er back to Portsmouth and living in sin with 'er.

EDIE (*with a little shriek*) 'En-ry!

HENRY. Emma really would appreciate that. So would Edie.

EDIE (*giggling*) Oh!

(ALBERT *lifts Edie*)

Albert!

(ALBERT *sits Edie on the table and crosses to* L *of it*)

Oh, Shirley, explain to him that he's married now. Baby still asleep?

SHIRLEY. Yes, Aunt Edie.

EDIE. 'E's the most beautiful baby I've ever seen.

ALBERT (*crossing to the fireplace; with pride*) That's what the Princess said, Aunt Edie. But I was forgetting——

(EMMA *enters from the kitchen, carrying a plate of cakes*)

—you don't know about that photograph.

EMMA. What photograph? (*She puts the plate on the table*) Edie, when your "sit-down" strike's over, p'raps you'll go into the kitchen and find them fairy cakes. *You* put 'em away, but the Lord knows where.

(EDIE *gets off the table and moves to the kitchen door*)

EDIE. Yes, Emma, Now, what did I . . . ? I remember giving one to 'Enry's ferrets.

EMMA. My fairy cakes for ferrets! What next will they want?

HENRY (*muttering*) Coffins.

(EDIE *exits to the kitchen*)

EMMA (*moving below the table*) And what's all this about photographs? What photograph—that is, if nobody minds *me* knowing.

ALBERT. Where is it, Shirl?

SHIRLEY. Upstairs. (*She rises*) I'll go and get it.

(SHIRLEY *exits to the hall*)

EMMA. What's it a photograph of—the baby?

ALBERT. Well—yes—in a way.

EMMA. What do you mean—"in a way"—is it or isn't it?

ALBERT. It's a photograph of the Princess looking at—(*he gestures towards the carry-cot*) his nibs.

EMMA (*moving* LC) The Princess?

ALBERT. You remember she visited the hospital on the day he was born?

EMMA (*sharply*) So did I, but I didn't get in.

ALBERT (*moving to* R *of Emma*) Er—no. It was unfortunate, that. But you know what it is—they seem as if they have to have all this red tape—security, and what not, when royalty are visiting.

HENRY. 'Course they 'ave. (*To Emma*) For all they knew, you might 'ave had a bomb in your bloomers.

ALBERT (*pointing to the carry-cot*) As his lordship was born about an hour before the Princess arrived, and as he was the first baby born in the new hospital, she was sort of intrigued, as you might say. Asked specially to see him.

(SHIRLEY *enters from the hall, carrying a photograph*)

Didn't she, Shirl?

SHIRLEY. Didn't who what?

ALBERT. I was just telling your mother about the Princess asking to see the baby.

(SHIRLEY *moves to* L *of Emma.* HENRY *rises and moves to* R *of Albert*)

SHIRLEY. Oh, yes. Ever so taken with him, they told me. This is a photograph of her looking at him. Pity you can only see his left leg. (*She hands the photograph to Emma*)

EMMA (*muttering*) I've never heard such . . . (*She studies the photograph*) Well, I don't like her 'at for a start.

(ALBERT *looks at* HENRY, *who gives him a big wink*)

H'mm! You say that's his *left* leg.

(ALBERT *crosses to the fireplace*)

Very nice, I'm sure. So is the Princess, come to that, but—that 'at!

SHIRLEY. Oh, Mum, she was wonderful. She was real interested in baby—(*to Albert*) wasn't she?

EMMA (*grudgingly*) Well, that's natural enough seeing that—(*she jerks her head towards Albert*) his father works for her sister.

HENRY (*moving to* R *of Emma; smiling*) I suppose she didn't hand him a knighthood, by any chance?

EMMA (*sharply*) That's enough from you. (*Sharper still*) And you might condescend to 'ave a look at this. (*She thrusts the photograph into Henry's hand*) If royalty can show an interest in your grandchild, I don't see why you should go scot free.

HENRY (*looking at the photograph*) Aye! (*Genuinely*) She's bonnie, isn't she? And what's the *matter* with her hat?

EMMA. I wouldn't like anyone to see *me* in it.

HENRY (*muttering*) Neither would I.

SHIRLEY. They say she looked lovely.

HENRY. Smashin'! . . . Pity she isn't comin' to the christening as well as . . . (*He pulls up quickly*)

EMMA (*in a flash*) As well as who?

HENRY. Er—the others.

(EMMA *looks suspiciously at* ALBERT *who turns to the fireplace.* HENRY *crosses behind Emma and stands above the sofa.* SHIRLEY *moves to* L *of the sofa.* HENRY *hands the photograph to Shirley*)

EMMA (*moving* C) What others? What's all this? (*To Albert*) Have you invited someone to the christening—someone I don't know about?

ALBERT (*turning and moving* RC; *with a suggestion of nervousness*) I—

er—I—we didn't exactly invite 'em, did we, Shirl? But they asked
if they could come, so naturally we . . .
EMMA. Who are you talking about?
SHIRLEY. Cousin Daphne, Mum, and her husband—Carnoustie.
EMMA (*in horror*) *Them?*
ALBERT (*firmly*) Them.
EMMA. You've invited them—after the things Daphne said to me
on your wedding day—after I told Daphne Pink I'd finished with
her for good and all?
SHIRLEY. But, Mum, Daphne is your own niece.
ALBERT. And Carnoustie is my best pal.
EMMA (*turning to Albert*) And I should keep *that* to yourself if I
were you.
SHIRLEY. And you didn't really mean what you said about
Daphne, now, did you?
EMMA. Have you ever known me talk just for the sake of talking?

(HENRY *chokes loudly over his pipe*)

(*She turns on Henry*) That's right! (*She rushes to the carry-cot and peers in*)
Blow smoke all over the poor little mite. Have him waking up
thinking the house is on fire. (*To Albert and Shirley*) Well—it's your
child that's being christened, so I *suppose* you can invite who you
like.
ALBERT (*moving to the fireplace; not without sarcasm*) Thank you,
Ma.
EMMA. But, Henry——
HENRY. Yes, Emma?
EMMA. —this is your house, isn't it?
HENRY (*blinking*) If you say so.
EMMA. I *do* say so. It's your house and it's for me to say who
you have in it.

(HENRY *crosses above the table to the easy chair and sits*)

(*She turns to Shirley*) When are they coming, these two? Tomorrow?
SHIRLEY (*moving to L of Emma*) No, Mum. Today.
EMMA. What? You mean they're staying overnight?
SHIRLEY. Well, you see, Carnoustie's got a "forty-eight" and as
we went to their baby's christening, it was only natural that they
should . . . (*She breaks off*)

(*There is a pause as* EMMA *paces up and down* c)

EMMA (*fuming*) Very natural, I *must* say. Very natural that,
without so much as by-your-leave you should expect me to house
and feed them—that 'eathen Scotchman and . . .
ALBERT (*moving to R of Emma; almost shouting her down*) We don't
expect anything of the sort.
EMMA. But if they're coming here . . .
ALBERT (*shortly*) They're *not*.
EMMA. You mean you 'aven't invited them here?

ALBERT (*moving to* R *of the table; it bursts out of him*) Of course not,
you silly old . . .
SHIRLEY (*horrified*) Albert!

(EMMA *gapes at Albert then crosses to* L *of Henry*)

EMMA (*at last; gasping*) Well, I . . . ! (*At a loss*) Henry . . .
HENRY. Yes?
EMMA (*suddenly regaining command*) Shut up! I'll handle this
myself. (*To Albert*) You'll explain that—statement, young man.
ALBERT (*still roused*) I mean that—in spite of what you might
think to the contrary, Ma—I have got *some* sense.
SHIRLEY (*moving to* L *of Albert; to Emma; anxiously*) He means he
wouldn't dream of asking them to come here without asking you
first—don't you, Albert?
ALBERT (*firmly*) No.
SHIRLEY (*deflated*) Oh!
ALBERT (*crossing below Emma to the fireplace*) I simply mean that
they're my friends, and as I'm very fond of both of them I wouldn't
dream of asking them to come here *at all*.
SHIRLEY (*moving* L) Albert!
EMMA (*ominously*) And why not, may I ask?
ALBERT (*unruffled, but firmly*) You know damn well why not, Ma,
and if you *don't*, then you *wouldn't* like to know. Now—shall we leave
it at that? But—if you like—I'm quite prepared to explain myself in
words of one syllable.
HENRY (*quietly*) They 'ave some 'orrible one-syllable words in the
Navy, Emma.

(EMMA *looks towards Albert as if she is prepared to give battle, but*
ALBERT *meets her glare firmly. There is quite a pause then* EMMA *moves
down* L *of the table.* SHIRLEY *goes to the carry-cot and bends over it.*
EDIE *bursts in from the kitchen, carrying a plate of fairy cakes*)

EDIE (*as she enters; brightly*) I've found the fairy cakes. You'll
never guess where.
HENRY. Do we 'ave to?

(EDIE *puts the cakes on the table and crosses to* R *of Shirley*)

EDIE. What about baby, Shirley? What about his tea?
SHIRLEY (*smiling*) Don't you worry, Aunt Edie. (*With a bigger
smile*) *I* feed him.
EDIE (*innocently and disappointedly*) Oh! Can't I do it?
HENRY (*muttering*) Stone the crows!
EMMA (*with a burst*) Edie 'Ornett, 'aven't you ever heard of the
acts of life at all?
EDIE (*bewildered*) But, Emma, I only . . . (*The light breaks through.
She is at once covered with confusion. She looks around at them all*) Oh-h!
'Scuse me, please.

(EDIE *flings up her apron and runs off to the kitchen*)

Henry. Poor old Edie. That's caught 'er well above the belt.

Emma (*moving to the kitchen door*) Henry! (*Shortly*) Tea'll be ready in five minutes. Oh, and while you're waiting you can look at that. (*She indicates the cot* L)

(Shirley *goes to the cot and looks at it*)

Shirley (*half pleased; half dismayed*) Oh, Mum . . .

Emma. I bought it for you this afternoon. 'Course, if I'd known all the facts I'd 'ave 'ad "By Royal Appointment" put on it.

(Emma *exits to the kitchen*)

Shirley (*crossing to Albert*) Albert Tufnell, I could kill you.

Albert (*crossing down* L) Now look, Shirl. I told you before we came what it would be like. There's as much chance of your mother and me hitting it off as there is of a couple of tomcats playin' tiddleywinks together.

Shirley. Oh, Dad, can't you talk to him; make him see sense?

Henry (*firmly*) Not on your Nelly.

Shirley. What?

Henry (*rising and moving to* R *of Shirley*) You fight your own battles. My fightin' days are over. I went out for the count about ten minutes after I'd married your mother, and I've taken damn good care to stay that way ever since.

(Henry *crosses and exits to the hall*)

Shirley (*turning on Albert; sharply*) Now, you listen to me, Albert. I'm not going to spend the whole week-end . . .

Albert (*overlapping*) And you listen to me. Let's get this straight. If you think I'm going to . . .

(*From the carry-cot comes a fairly long wail which silences them. They look towards the carry-cot for a moment*)

(*He smiles*) Pipped at the post!

Shirley (*sitting on the sofa beside the carry-cot*) It's all right, my darling, mother's here.

Albert (*moving to the carry-cot; smiling*) I'm here, too.

(Shirley *takes a toy from the carry-cot*)

Shirley. Hold that a second.

Albert (*taking the toy*) Bit of a psychologist, this son of ours.

Shirley (*busy straightening the covers*) Now what are you talking about?

Albert. Must have been listening; knew damn well we were spoiling for a row, and he wasn't going to have that. (*He speaks into the carry-cot*) Hate rows, don't you, Son? I don't blame you. I hate 'em, too. (*He looks hopefully at Shirley for a moment*)

(Shirley *continues straightening the carry-cot*)

(*He talks to the toy*) And you don't like 'em either, do you, Jinxy?
'Course you don't. Senseless sort of things, aren't they?

SHIRLEY (*taking the toy from Albert*) Do you mind? Unless, of
course, you're waiting for an answer. (*She puts the toy into the carry-
cot*)

ALBERT. Darling. Getting him up now?

SHIRLEY (*quietly*) No. He's going off again. May as well leave
him until after tea—if he'll stay.

(ALBERT *moves to the cot* L)

ALBERT (*making conversation*) H'mm! Bit dodgy about this, isn't
it? I mean—she'll have to be told—won't she? Doesn't seem much
point in having two cots—exactly the same make. 'Tisn't as if we'd
got twins. (*He pauses*) Who's going to tell her—you or me?

SHIRLEY (*uncomfortably*) Oh, dear!

ALBERT. Dodgy!

SHIRLEY (*with a touch of irritation*) I wish she'd asked me before
buying it. If she'd bought us a *pram* . . .

ALBERT. And we don't want a pram, either.

SHIRLEY. No. I know. But . . .

ALBERT. We're not allowed to have one in the flat. Besides—
getting it up all those stairs.

SHIRLEY. I'm not *arguing* with you—all I'm saying is, mum
might have guessed we had a cot already.

ALBERT (*crossing below the sofa to* C; *quietly*) It was a kind thought,
anyway.

SHIRLEY. Just a waste of good money.

ALBERT (*perching on the downstage edge of the table*) But still—a kind
thought. (*He looks up suddenly, surprised, then bursts into loud laughter*)

SHIRLEY (*not angrily*) Albert, what on earth . . . ? Ssssh!

(ALBERT *stops laughing*)

ALBERT. Sorry.

SHIRLEY. What's tickling you?

ALBERT (*quietly, but with laughter in his voice*) I suddenly realized
I was sticking up for your mother.

SHIRLEY (*laughing*) Oh, Albert!

ALBERT. I must be crackers. Stark staring bonkers.

(SHIRLEY *suddenly rises and rushes to Albert*)

SHIRLEY. You're wonderful!

ALBERT (*blinking*) Eh?

SHIRLEY (*putting her arms around him*) The most wonderful, most
kind-hearted person in the world.

ALBERT (*happily*) Oi! Come off it.

SHIRLEY. And I'm—I'm . . . Why don't you turn me upside down
and give me a good spanking?

ALBERT. That's an idea! Why don't I? (*He twirls Shirley around
and pulls her across his lap*)

(HENRY *enters from the hall*)

SHIRLEY. Albert! No!

(HENRY *crosses to* L *of Albert*)

ALBERT (*with hand raised*) Now who's the boss?

(HENRY *crosses to* R *of the table.* ALBERT *releases Shirley and moves below the sofa.* SHIRLEY *sits on the right arm of the sofa*)

HENRY (*looking towards the kitchen door*) Why didn't *I* learn judo?
ALBERT. You arrived in the nick of time, Pop. I was just going to give your daughter a spanking.
HENRY (*moving to the fireplace*) Then I reckon I arrived too early.
SHIRLEY. Dad!

(EDIE *enters from the kitchen carrying a tray with large plates, food, etc.*)

EDIE (*as she enters*) Tea'll be in in a minute.
HENRY. This tea's like the ruddy Campbells—always "coming" but never arrives.
EDIE (*setting out the plates and food on the table*) Emma'll be here in a minute, too.
HENRY (*sitting in the easy chair; murmuring*) Loud cheers.
EDIE. She's just washing her hands.
HENRY. We can do without the commentary, Mr Dimbleby.

(ALBERT *guffaws.*
    EMMA *enters from the kitchen and moves down* C. ALBERT *swallows his laughter immediately. At once everyone sobers up*)

EMMA. Edie, I thought I told you to get the chairs up to the table.
EDIE. Yes, Emma. (*She puts the empty tray on the floor beside the sideboard, collects the chair* R *of the window and puts it below the left end of the table*)
EMMA (*to Shirley*) Well?
SHIRLEY (*rising; puzzled*) Well what, Mum?

(EDIE *collects the chair* L *of the window and sets it* L *of the table, then rearranges the food on the table*)

EMMA. Have you decided what you think about it—both of you?

(EDIE *puts a bowl of tomatoes on the chair below the left end of the table*)

SHIRLEY (*still not understanding*) What, Mum? I don't know what you're talking about.
ALBERT (*to Shirley; under his breath*) The cot!
EMMA (*crossing to the cot* L) Oh, well, of course, if you're not interested I might as well have saved my money.
SHIRLEY (*crossing to Emma*) It's a lovely cot, but—er . . .

EDIE (*getting the hang of the conversation*) Oh .Emma, you 'aven't shown them yours, already!

EMMA (*sharply*) Quiet, you! (*To Shirley*) So it should be a lovely cot—the price it was. Eight pounds ten.

ALBERT. Eight pounds seven and six at Portsmouth.

EMMA. What?

ALBERT. That's what we paid, isn't it, Shirl, for the one we bought; same make; same pattern exactly.

SHIRLEY. Of course, if we'd known you . . .

(EMMA *stands glaring at Albert for a moment then crosses to the sideboard and takes a bill from her handbag*)

EMMA. Henry!

HENRY. What?

EMMA (*moving to L of Henry*) Berrington's Stores'll be closed by the time we've had tea, but first thing tomorrow morning you'll take that—(*she points to the cot*) straight back there and tell them we don't want it.

HENRY (*protesting*) Here—look—I didn't buy it.

EMMA (*ignoring Henry's protests and handing him the bill*) Here's the bill—eight pounds ten I paid, and—(*she moves to R of the table and thumps on it*) eight pounds ten you want back. Understand?

HENRY. But—what excuse can I make?

EMMA (*moving below the table*) You don't want an excuse. What you want is eight pounds ten. And when you've got it you can tell them they're nothing but thieves and robbers; that you can get the same thing in Portsmouth for eight pounds seven and six.

(EDIE *moves the tomatoes as* EMMA *nearly sits on the chair down* L *of the table*)

HENRY. I'm going to be popular!

(EMMA *crosses to the cot* L. EDIE *puts the bowl of tomatoes on the table, pushes the chair under the table then crosses to the chair down* R)

EMMA (*taking the golliwog from the cot*) And this had better go, too. (*She speaks at Albert, but not to him*) Two pounds ten, this was. (*She moves* C *and tosses the golliwog to Henry*) But I expect they're sixpence a dozen at Portsmouth.

(HENRY *tosses the golliwog back to* EMMA *who throws it into his lap*)

HENRY (*muttering*) I'm going to look a proper Charley.

EMMA. In future—speaking for myself at any rate—I shall keep my nose out of things that don't concern me.

HENRY (*quietly*) Time'll drag.

EMMA (*crossing down* L) But I should like it put on record that what I did I did for the best. And I can't say more than that, can I?

HENRY (*muttering*) What's the betting?

(EDIE *picks up the chair down* R *and crosses towards the table*)

EMMA. Right! Then that's settled. (*She indicates the cot*) This thing goes out of here tomorrow morning. (*She goes up* L *and drags the wooden cradle down* C) And that goes for this, too.

EDIE (*with a little whimper*) Oh—Emma . . .

EMMA (*overlapping*) Whatever you paid for it, Edie, it's a pity, 'cos I expect, in Portsmouth, these things are given away with a packet of tea.

(EDIE *puts down the chair, sits on it, gives a loud howl and sobs*)

SHIRLEY (*rushing to Edie*) What is it, Aunt Edie?

EMMA. A waste of good money, that's what it is.

HENRY (*rising, crossing to* C *and blinking at the cradle*) What the 'ell's it supposed to . . . ? (*To Edie. Irritably*) Pipe down, Edie, for the Lord's sake. (*He looks at the cradle*) Where did it come from?

EMMA. Ask Edie. *She* bought it.

SHIRLEY (*gaping at the cradle*) You bought that for—for . . . ? Oh, no, Aunt Edie.

(EDIE *howls long and loud*)

(*She tries to shout Edie down*) It was very kind of you, Aunt Edie, but —really . . . !

(EDIE's *howls dissolve into low sobs*)

(*She crosses to Albert*) We do appreciate the thought, don't we, Albert?

ALBERT (*heavily*) Yeah!

HENRY (*bending and inspecting the cradle*) Been a bit of good wood.

(EDIE *gives a little moan*)

Riddled wi' worm.

(EDIE *howls*)

Bet this wasn't made yesterday; nor the day before.

EDIE (*between sobs*) It's antique.

HENRY. Oh, it's older than that.

EDIE (*in jerks*) The man at the shop said Mary Queen of Scots hid her baby in it—on Mafeking Night.

HENRY. And you believed him?

EMMA. *Believed* him? She'd have believed him if he'd told her the Queen of Sheba'd spent her honeymoon in it. But no matter who slept in it, when or where, it's either going back where it came from or it goes out to the coalhouse to be chopped up for firewood. (*To Edie*) Do you want to take it back?

EDIE (*gulping*) No, Emma. It doesn't matter. (*She rises, picks up her chair, takes it down* R *and sits on it*)

EMMA. Then—Henry?

HENRY (*fearing the worst*) What? You're not going to get me to . . .

EMMA. Get this out into the coalhouse.
HENRY. What—right away?
EMMA. You just said it's full of worms, didn't you? Well, we all know what worms are—worse than rabbits. Before we can turn round the whole *house'll* be *full* of worms. Out with it.
HENRY (*grumbling*) I should've thought we might 'ave got tea over first.
EMMA (*with a burst of angry impatience*) Oh, for goodness' sake, sit down. I'll take it out myself.

(HENRY *crosses to the fireplace*)

(*She picks up the cradle and moves towards the kitchen door*) But don't forget—the minute you get back from Berrington's tomorrow morning, you get your jacket off and into the coalhouse, and if this thing isn't chopped up by . . .
ALBERT (*suddenly; quietly but authoritatively*) Just a minute, Ma.
EMMA (*after the slightest pause*) Now what?
ALBERT (*to Edie; quietly*) Aunt Edie.
EDIE (*timorously*) Yes, Albert?
ALBERT. You bought that cradle for Shirl and me, didn't you?
EDIE (*rising*) I—I . . .
ALBERT. You did, didn't you?
EDIE (*moving* RC; *wretchedly*) But I didn't know about the worms, Albert. You see, I thought . . .
ALBERT (*kindly but firmly*) Never mind about the worms. Aunt Edie. You bought it for us, didn't you?
EDIE (*crossing to* R *of Albert; with a scared look at Emma*) Yes, Albert, I—I . . .
ALBERT. And are you still giving it to us?
EDIE (*now in a complete dither*) But you can't want it—can you? I mean, you don't want baby playing with worms.

(SHIRLEY, *seeing trouble ahead, moves to* L *of Albert*)

SHIRLEY (*anxiously*) Just a minute, Aunt Edie. (*To Albert. Pleading*) Albert, what are you up to now?
ALBERT (*quietly*) Keep out of this, Shirl.

(SHIRLEY *moves* L. ALBERT *puts* EDIE *across him to* LC *and moves to* L *of Emma.* HENRY *sits in the easy chair*)

SHIRLEY. You're not going to start anything?
EMMA (*ominously*) I should like to know what this is all about.
ALBERT (*quietly*) You will, Ma. (*Firmly*) What I'm trying to do is establish right of ownership. (*He raises his voice a little*) Is that cradle mine or isn't it—that's all I want to know, and it's as simple as that. Aunt Edie?
EDIE (*desperately*) Of course it's yours, if you really . . .
ALBERT. Fine! Now we know where we stand. (*To Emma. Quietly*) Ma—(*he moves to Emma with outstretched arms*) can I have my property, please?

EMMA. I don't know what you think you're playing at, young man.

ALBERT. All I'm doing is asking you to hand over what belongs to me.

EMMA. Before I'd let you put my grandchild in this worm-ridden thing, I'd send for the whole of the Royal Society for Prevention of Cruelty to Children.

HENRY (*quietly*) I shouldn't bother, Emma; a tin of Flit . . .

ALBERT (*quietly*) Ma, I don't want to lose my temper.

EMMA. No, but you're trying your best to make me lose mine, aren't you?

ALBERT (*quieter still*) Can I have my property, please? (*He puts his hands on the cradle*)

(EMMA *swings bodily away releasing Albert's light hold*)

EMMA (*fuming*) Henry, are you going to sit there . . . ?

HENRY. Right here. (*Quietly*) I couldn't do any good—Albert's within his rights.

ALBERT. Thanks, Pop.

SHIRLEY (*almost in tears*) But, Dad, he doesn't want the cradle. You know that as well as I do.

EDIE (*wailing*) Oh, why did I buy it?

ALBERT (*holding out his arms*) Ma?

(EMMA *drops the cradle to the floor*)

EMMA. All right, then—take it—if it's yours, take it.

ALBERT (*picking up the cradle; quietly*) If there are any worms in there you'll have killed them.

EMMA. But you'll get it out of my house, right away, d'y' hear?

ALBERT. I hear. (*He looks around*) Where's my cap?

SHIRLEY (*near to panic*) Albert! Where are you . . . ? What are you . . . ? Albert, you're not *going?*

ALBERT. Ma's just told me to.

SHIRLEY. But *where* are you going?

ALBERT. Where *is* my cap? (*He moves down* C)

EDIE (*crossing to the hall door*) Albert! You're not going—deserting your wife and innocent child? Albert, you can't do it; not for a few worms.

(ALBERT *moves to the window, looking for his cap.* SHIRLEY *follows him to* R *of the sofa. There is a loud and long wail from the carry-cot*)

EMMA (*moving towards the carry-cot; to Edie*) *Now* look what you've done.

SHIRLEY (*moving towards the carry-cot*) It's all right, my darling. Mother's . . .

(EDIE *forestalls Shirley and Emma and reaches the carry-cot first.* ALBERT *crosses above the table to the sideboard*)

Edie (*kneeling beside the carry-cot*) No, Shirley, no! Let me! You stop Albert.

(Shirley *crosses to Albert*)

He mustn't desert his wife and child.

(*The front-door bell rings*)

Emma. Edie! The front door.

(Edie *is now crooning, or rather yelling, to the baby in the carry-cot*)

Edie (*clapping her hands in time with her "singing"*)
> "London Bridge is falling down,
> Falling down, falling down,
> London Bridge is falling down . . ."

Emma (*trying to top Edie*) Edie, do I have to go and answer it?

(*The front-door bell rings*)

(*Furiously*) Oh, all right.

(Emma, *exasperated, exits to the hall.* Albert *moves down* R)

Edie (*louder and wilder*)
> "London Bridge is falling down,
> Falling down . . ."

(*The baby yells loudly.* Shirley, *torn between anxiety for the baby's welfare and Albert's intentions, follows him down* R)

Albert (*finding his cap; with satisfaction*) Ah!
Shirley. Albert, you've got to tell me. Where *are* you going?
Albert (*crossing to* C *and shouting to top Edie*) The station.
Shirley (*crossing to* R *of Albert*) Albert! (*Desperately*) The christening! You can't mean—you're going home?
Albert. I'm not.
Shirley. But you said—the station.
Albert. Yeah. The left luggage office. (*He pats the cradle and crosses to the hall door*) Be seeing you.

(Emma *enters from the hall.* Albert *retreats to* LC. Emma *slams the door*)

Emma (*bearing down on Albert; for once, almost bereft of speech*) You —you . . . ! Ooooh!
Albert (*backing down* R) What the . . . ?
Emma (*her voice throbbing with fury*) And you had the nerve to tell me—to say—to swear . . . Ooooooh!
Henry (*feebly*) But, Emma . . .
Shirley (*moving to* R *of Emma*) Mum, what is it?

(Emma *brushes Shirley aside to* R *of the sofa*)

Emma (*beginning to "flay" Albert*) Of all the downright . . . ! (*With fine scorn*) *You* 'adn't invited 'em here. Oh, no, not you! You wouldn't dream of inviting them, would you? They were your friends and you were too fond of 'em to . . .

ALBERT (*in horror*) You don't mean . . . ?

EMMA (*topping him*) That's *just* what I mean; and well you know it. They're out there—cluttering up my hall with . . . (*She rushes to the hall door, flings it wide open and calls loudly*) In here, the pair of you.

(DAPHNE BLIGH *enters from the hall. She is a smart, streamlined young matron of Shirley's age, with a charming manner and, though not at the moment, an attractive smile. She is carrying a small suitcase, a large doll and a carry-cot. From the entrance of Daphne the scene is played at tremendous pace with much overlapping of dialogue*)

DAPHNE (*as she enters; troubled*) Aunt Emma, I do assure you . . .

(HENRY *rises*)

SHIRLEY (*gaping*) Daphne!

ALBERT (*weakly*) Daphne! (*He puts the cradle on the floor down* R)

(DAPHNE "*takes*" *Shirley and Albert and crosses to Shirley. She and* SHIRLEY *move up* C.

CARNOUSTIE BLIGH *enters from the hall. He, like Albert, is in naval uniform and again, like him, has his manly beauty, but it inclines to be severe. He takes life very seriously and speaks with a Scottish brogue. He carries a suitcase, a small pillow, a small rug, and on the crook of one arm, a small baby*)

CARNOUSTIE (*as he enters*) Och, I'm sorry, Mrs Hornett—we dinna want to cause ye any trouble.

ALBERT (*weakly*) Carnoustie! And the baby, too. Oh, my God!

(CARNOUSTIE *crossing to* L *of Daphne*)

EDIE (*wildly*)
> "Little Miss Muffet,
> Sat on a tuffet,
> Eating her curds and whey . . ."

HENRY (*moving* RC; *trying to make himself heard*) 'Ullo, there! Nice to see you.

EMMA (*crossing to* C *and turning on Henry*) Nice? *Nice?* It isn't nice at all. It's far *from* nice! I've been tricked—deceived . . .

EDIE (*through this*)
> "There came a big spider
> Who sat down beside her . . ."

EMMA (*at striking point*) *Edie!* Will you . . . ?

(*Carnoustie's baby now begins to yell*)

Listen! Did you ever hear . . . ?

(DAPHNE *drops all she is carrying and quickly takes the baby from Carnoustie*)

DAPHNE (*rocking the baby*) There, there, my lamb . . .

Carnoustie (*hovering over the baby; anxiously*) She'll be all right, Mrs Hornett. If ye could just no' shout so much . . .

(Edie *rises, with her back to the audience*)

Emma (*pacing to and fro* c; *boiling*) Me! Shout! My house turned into a maternity home. Cots here, cradles there—babies everywhere . . .

(Edie, *scarcely conscious of the others, takes Shirley's baby from the carry-cot in a very inexperienced manner, turns, and jerkily rocks the baby*)

Edie (*loudly and rocking with abandon*)
                "And frightened Miss Muffet
                    away—ay!"
Emma. *Edie* You've got it *upside down!*
Edie. Have I? Oh!

Emma *takes the baby from Edie as*—

the Curtain *falls*

ACT II

SCENE I

SCENE—*The same. The following morning.*

When the CURTAIN *rises, it is about nine o'clock.* HENRY *is down* LC, *parcelling up the cot that Emma bought. He is struggling with two large pieces of brown paper and a length of string.* ALBERT, *minus his blouse, is combing his hair at the mirror over the mantelpiece.*

HENRY. Bloody thing!

ALBERT (*smiling*) T', t', t'! Language, Pop. And in front of your son-in-law.

HENRY (*growling*) I'd like to ring my son-in-law's neck.

ALBERT (*with a heavy sigh*) I wonder if I'd mind.

HENRY (*accusingly but jokingly*) I suppose you know this barney is all your fault? Telling Edie you wanted that cradle of hers when you didn't really want it at all.

ALBERT (*embarrassed*) Oh, that!

HENRY. Never mind "Oh, that-ing," it was nice of you. It's made Edie really 'appy; made 'er forget 'er "great sorrow" for once. And—for what it's worth—I appreciate it, Son. (*He struggles with the parcel. Irritably*) Oh, blast it!

ALBERT (*crossing to Henry*) Just what are you trying to do?

HENRY. I'm trying to get this ruddy thing parcelled up and out of sight before Emma comes down again. I suppose I'll 'ave to take it back to Berringtons.

ALBERT. Now, look, why don't you sit down and have a smoke and let the Navy handle this?

HENRY (*with alacrity*) Aye, aye, sir. (*He salutes and crosses to the fireplace*) I suppose the Navy wouldn't think of taking it back to Berringtons and asking for eight pounds ten? (*He turns*)

ALBERT. You're right; it wouldn't. (*He continues with the parcelling*)

HENRY. Oh! (*He sits in the easy chair, takes out his pipe, fills and lights it*)

ALBERT. I wonder what sort of a night Carnoustie and Daphne had next door at Mrs Lack's. I haven't heard them about; have you?

HENRY. Florrie Lack isn't what you'd call an early riser.

ALBERT (*still busy with the parcel*) Can't understand that, myself. I *like* to be up early—fresh air . . .

HENRY (*after a snort*) Fresh air and Florrie aren't on speaking terms.

(*The kitchen door is opened cautiously.*
CARNOUSTIE's *head appears round the kitchen door*)

CARNOUSTIE (*in a hoarse, and almost sinister whisper*) Albert!

HENRY (*leaping up in alarm*) What the . . . ? (*He moves to the kitchen door. With a gasp of relief*) You frightened the life out of me.

CARNOUSTIE (*stepping into the room; solemnly*) Oh! Can a' come in?

HENRY (*bringing Carnoustie in*) Come in, lad. (*He closes the door then sits in the easy chair*)

CARNOUSTIE (*looking around apprehensively*) But—Mrs Hornett . . .

HENRY. She'll be buzzing around upstairs for a while yet. Sit yourself doon—er—down.

CARNOUSTIE. No, I'll no' do that. That'd be tempting Providence. I'll keep on ma' feet if ye dinna' mind. Aye, and—(*he moves to the kitchen door*) I'll have the door open ready. (*He opens the door, then moves to* L *of Henry*) Mind—I *want* to see Mrs Hornett—er—sometime.

HENRY (*blinking*) You do?

CARNOUSTIE. I want to apologize to her for all the inconvenience we caused.

HENRY. You did, last night—four times.

CARNOUSTIE. Aye, but I don't think she was listening.

HENRY. No. Emma's not good at that.

CARNOUSTIE. She seemed to be labouring under a misapprehension.

HENRY. She's *very* good at that.

CARNOUSTIE. She seemed to think Albert had invited us to come and stay *here*.

ALBERT (*grimly*) She still does.

CARNOUSTIE (*crossing to* R *of Albert; plaintively*) But I tried to tell her we'd been to the *Rose and Crown* and couldna' get in. All we wanted was an address we might try.

ALBERT (*grinning*) Well, you've got one.

CARNOUSTIE (*heavily*) Aye!

HENRY (*smiling*) How did you get on at Florrie's?

CARNOUSTIE (*moving to* R *of the table*) Have *you* ever slept on a mattress stuffed wi' walnuts?

HENRY. Never.

CARNOUSTIE. Neither had I—(*he is about to sit on the edge of the table but leaps up*) until last night.

HENRY. But did you have a good breakfast?

CARNOUSTIE (*cheering up*) Och, aye! The breakfast was fine.

ALBERT. You're joking.

CARNOUSTIE. My Daphne cooked it.

HENRY. *What?*

CARNOUSTIE. After she'd been out and bought it.

HENRY. D'you mean to say . . . ?

CARNOUSTIE. Weel—ye see—Mistress Lack doesna' exactly rise wi' the lark.

HENRY. Lark? No self-respecting lark would *let* her.

CARNOUSTIE. And as there wasna' anything to speak of in the larder, and as Mistress Lack's bairn was greetin' for summat tae eat . . .

Henry (*almost bursting*) You mean—*you've* fed that lazy trollop's kid for her?
Carnoustie. Aye—and *her*, as well.
Albert. *What?*
Carnoustie. Daphne took her breakfast up on a tray.
Henry (*rising*) My God! If Emma hears of this.
Albert. Don't let her hear it, Pop, for goodness' sake—not till we've got this christening over. (*He finishes the parcel and crosses to Henry*) There we are—all shipshape and Bristol fashion. What are you going to do with it?
Henry (*fuming*) I'd like to crack it down on Florrie Lack's head. (*He takes the parcel*)

(Albert *crosses and sits on the sofa at the left end*)

(*Without hope*) Carnoustie—you wouldn't be wanting a cot—cheap —*seven* pounds ten?
Carnoustie. No. We bought an expensive one—six pounds five.
Henry (*moving to the kitchen door*) It was just a thought.

(Henry *exits with the parcel to the kitchen*)

Carnoustie (*moving to the kitchen door and speaking off*) A' would have liked to oblige you, Mr Hornett, but you know how it is. (*He checks that the door is open, then moves below the table and perches on the end of it. He gives a long look at Albert*) How is she this morning?
Albert. How's who?
Carnoustie (*jerking his thumb towards the hall door*) Her—Mrs Hornett.
Albert (*grimly*) She wasn't too bad at breakfast; never came to the boil; just sat simmering.
Carnoustie. Och!

(*There is a pause.* Albert *takes out a packet of cigarettes and a box of matches*)

Albert. Smoke? (*He takes a cigarette for himself*)

(Carnoustie *takes out a small tin and a box of matches*)

Carnoustie (*taking a dog-end from the tin*) No, no. I hae this left over from last night.

(Albert *lights his cigarette.* Carnoustie *sees Albert with the lighted match, puts his own matches away, rises, crosses to the sofa and gets a light from Albert*)

Thanks! (*He sits* R *of Albert on the sofa, and rubs his nose*)
Albert. Don't worry, I'll save this butt for you as well.
Carnoustie. Where's Shirley? What's she up to?
Albert (*absently*) She's upstairs, bathing the baby.
Carnoustie. Uh-huh! And what about you?
Albert (*still absently*) I'm downstairs talking to you.

Carnoustie (*looking at Albert*) Uh-huh! (*He does a double-take as he realizes what Albert has said*)

(*They smoke silently for a while*)

Albert. How's Daphne?
Carnoustie (*after a look*) Och, she's fine.
Albert (*after a slight pause*) And the youngster?
Carnoustie. She's fine, too.
Albert (*vaguely*) That's fine.
Carnoustie. But you're no'.
Albert. What?
Carnoustie. Fine.
Albert (*muttering*) No, I'm no'—not.
Carnoustie (*after a slight pause*) What?
Albert. Fine.
Carnoustie. Oh! (*He pinches out his cigarette and puts it in the tin*)
Albert. Shirl and me have had a row.
Carnoustie (*distressed*) Dear, dear, dear!
Albert (*with a laugh*) A row! Two rows—three—I've lost count. We hadn't been in this ruddy house ten minutes before we had the first, and we've been having 'em at intervals ever since. It's only when we come up here—something seems to happen to Shirl. (*He rises and crosses to* rc)

(Edie *enters up* l *outside the window and crosses to* r. *She carries a basket of groceries*)

Carnoustie. Are ye sure it only happens to Shirley?
Albert (*moving down* r) What do you mean?
Carnoustie. Is it no' possible that it happens to you as well?

(Edie *appears at the open kitchen door. She is about to burst into her usual entrance babble, but realizing Carnoustie is speaking, refrains from doing so. When she hears what he is saying she retires into the kitchen, removing her hat as she does so. She does not close the door, and occasionally she is seen moving around in the kitchen.* Albert *and* Carnoustie *have not noticed her*)

Albert (*with a little laugh*) Quite the psychiatrist, aren't you, Son?
Carnoustie. Oh—I wouldna' say that.
Albert (*moving to* r *of the sofa*) And you're dead right, what's more. I have done something pretty lousy. (*He pauses briefly*) Did you happen to notice that wooden cradle I was carrying when you arrived last night?
Carnoustie (*with a little laugh*) Aye, I did.
Albert (*leaning over to him*) Aunt Edie bought it for us.
Carnoustie. Och! (*Quietly*) But you canna' possibly use it.
Albert (*with slight irritation*) 'Course we can't. But if you'd heard the way Ma just told Pop to get it out of the house and chopped up for firewood . . .

Carnoustie (*muttering*) That's aboot all it's good for.

Albert (*with a burst*) I know that. But that's not the point. Aunt Edie had given the thing to me—to *us*. It had sweet Fanny Adams to do with Ma—and I just saw red. I went for her; told her it was mine; I wanted it and I was going to have it. (*He crosses to the fireplace*) Now I'm landed with the damn thing and I suppose I'll have to cart it back to Portsmouth. (*He moves to the table and perches on it*) And now I've got Pop thinking me a hell of a feller for not hurting Aunt Edie's feelings, and—and this makes me feel a right bastard—there's poor Aunt Edie thinks I'm taking her ruddy cradle 'cos I really want it.

(Daphne *enters up* l *outside the window, crosses and goes into the kitchen*)

Daphne (*off; in the kitchen*) I've lost a husband, Aunt Edie.

(Albert *rises, crosses and sits* l *of Carnoustie on the sofa*)

Carnoustie. Och, here's Daphne.

(Edie *appears at the kitchen door.*
Daphne *follows her in*)

Edie (*rather quietly*) Carnoustie's in here, Daphne, with Albert. (*She gives a little sniff and dabs her eyes*)
Daphne. Anything wrong, Aunt Edie?
Edie (*bravely*) No, love. Emma's ever so calm today—for her, so everything's wonderful—(*she dabs her eyes*) wonderful.

(Edie *exits quickly to the kitchen.* Carnoustie *rises.* Daphne *looks after Edie then moves to* r *of the sofa*)

Daphne (*to Carnoustie*) So this is where you're hiding yourself. I thought you were supposed to be doing the washing-up? 'Morning, Albert.
Albert. 'Morning, Daphne.
Daphne. Where's Shirley—upstairs?
Albert. Yes.
Carnoustie (*looking apprehensively towards the hall door*) And Mrs Hornett's up there, too.
Daphne (*smiling*) So what?
Carnoustie (*taking Daphne's arm and leading her* c) We ought to get oot before she comes doon—that's what. Come away. (*He turns to Albert*) Albert, what you doing this morning?
Albert. I dunno. Why?
Carnoustie. I was thinking you and I might have a wee walk oot on our ain.
Daphne (*smiling*) Oh, yes?
Carnoustie. Aye. Ye've no objection, wumman?
Daphne. Oh, no. *I* haven't. But I'm quite sure someone will.
Albert (*rising and moving to* l *of Carnoustie*) I don't think Shirl

would mind if she never saw me again. (*He gives a little grin and crosses to the fireplace*) Well, not for quite a while, anyway.

(DAPHNE *and* CARNOUSTIE *exchange glances*)

DAPHNE. Yes, I think it would be a very good idea for you two to get out for a bit. (*She moves down* LC *and turns*) I'll keep Shirley company. (*She smiles at Albert*) Perhaps you ought to finish dressing first.

(ALBERT *moves to the chair down* R *and picks up his blouse.*
EMMA *and* SHIRLEY *enter from the hall.* EMMA *crosses to* C. SHIRLEY *crosses to* L *of Daphne.* ALBERT *has his blouse over his head*)

CARNOUSTIE (*with a yelp*) Ma' God! (*He dives for the kitchen door*)
EMMA (*almost as she enters*) Now then, now then! What's going on? How long have you two been here?
DAPHNE. Just a few minutes, Aunt Emma.

(ALBERT *turns to the mirror over the fireplace and arranges his blouse, etc.*)

EMMA (*to Daphne*) How did you get on last night at Florrie Lack's?
DAPHNE (*moving to* R *of the sofa*) Oh, very well—didn't we, Carnoustie? It was very kind of you to fix us there.
EMMA. Well, I 'ad to do something, didn't I? (*She glares at Albert*) 'Course, if I'd been told *straight out*, in the first place, that you were coming here, I might've arranged something different. It gave me no pleasure, I can tell you, 'aving to go to Florrie Lack and plead and grovel to get you put up.
CARNOUSTIE (*moving up to* L *of Emma; beginning to boil*) Now look here, Mrs Hornett, I'm sorry if . . .
EMMA (*overriding him*) But we'll say no more about it. (*With a gesture of impatience*) Well, get yourselves sat down, since you *are* here.

(CARNOUSTIE *glares. He and* DAPHNE *sidle to the sofa and sit,* CARNOUSTIE R *of Daphne.* SHIRLEY *sits on the left arm of the sofa.* EMMA *looks at Albert, then looks back at the sofa as* CARNOUSTIE, DAPHNE *and* SHIRLEY *smile nervously*)

CARNOUSTIE (*rising*) We were just thinking of . . .
EMMA. There's no need for you to think of anything; that's my 'eadache.

(CARNOUSTIE *resumes his seat*)

(*To Daphne. Sharply*) Where's *your* child?
DAPHNE. Outside in the garden.
EMMA (*sharper*) Whose garden—not Florrie Lack's?
DAPHNE. No, I brought her round into yours. I hope you don't mind, Aunt Emma.
EMMA. If you'd left it in 'ers, I'd 'ave reported you. Shirley,

why don't you put baby out in the garden with Daphne's; it'll be nice for them.

ALBERT (*moving* RC) Why will it?

EMMA (*turning to Albert; nonplussed*) They can look at each other.

SHIRLEY. I'll fetch him down.

ALBERT (*crossing to the hall door*) I'll do it.

SHIRLEY (*with some asperity*) There's no need for you to . . .

ALBERT (*firmly*) I'll do it.

(ALBERT *exits to the hall*)

EMMA (*looking after Albert*) Well, I dunno! We're always hearing about "jolly Jack Tars", but if he's a fair sample . . . (*She picks up the brush and crumb tray from the table, moves above the table and brushes up the crumbs*)

(EDIE, *red-eyed and sniffing, enters from the kitchen and stands in the doorway*)

(*To Edie. Almost accusingly*) Well?

EDIE (*whimpering*) I'm back.

EMMA (*heavily*) That's nice, isn't it? Now we can 'ave a party.

EDIE (*blinking*) What, *before* the christening, as well?

EMMA (*indulgently*) I was bein' 'umorous, Edie. 'Course, you wouldn't understand. (*She goes to the sideboard and puts down the brush and crumb tray*)

(EDIE *moves down* R)

SHIRLEY (*rising and crossing to Edie*) Don't tease Aunt Edie, Mum. Aunt Edie, have you been crying?

EDIE (*brokenly*) No—no . . .

SHIRLEY. You *have*, you know.

EDIE (*wildly*) No, I haven't—I've been getting dinner ready— onions . . .

EMMA (*moving to* R *of Edie; expostulating*) Onions! Edie, we're not 'aving onions with boiled cod. (*Accusingly*) Is it your "great sorrow" again, 'cos if it is . . .

EDIE. It isn't, Emma. (*Bravely*) It's nothing—nothing at all. (*She makes a gesture of wiping all sorrow from her face and faces them with a rather ghastly forced smile*) There—see. (*She holds the smile*)

(*They all look at Edie*)

EMMA (*crossing to the table and removing the breakfast cloth*) Yes, well, that's quite enough of *that*.

(SHIRLEY *moves to the fireplace*)

EDIE (*crossing to* R *of the sofa*) Daphne, your baby—little Penny-lope . . .

DAPHNE (*not unkindly*) "Penelope", Aunt Edie.

EDIE (*almost unheeding*) Your little Pen—what-you-said—looks ever so sweet lying in her cot in the garden,

CARNOUSTIE (*delighted*) Och—thank you, Aunt Edie.
EDIE. Have you seen her, Emma?
EMMA. No.
EDIE. Lovely she looks. (*Brokenly*) Beautiful. Makes you feel you want to *eat* her. And there's Mrs Mottram's cat sitting on the fence—just looking; can't take his eyes off her.
CARNOUSTIE (*leaping into action*) What? (*He dashes to the kitchen door*)
EDIE (*following him; explaining*) Oh, I don't think he's hungry.
CARNOUSTIE. My God!

(CARNOUSTIE *exits to the kitchen*)

EDIE. He's only *looking*, Carnoustie.

(EDIE *exits to the kitchen*)

EMMA (*crossing to the sideboard*) The times I've told Maisie Mottram . . . (*She puts the tablecloth on the sideboard*)

(ALBERT *enters from the hall, carrying the blue carry-cot*)

ALBERT (*to Shirley*) I'll put him out in the garden, so's they can look at each other.

(ALBERT *exits to the kitchen with the carry-cot.*
     SHIRLEY *follows Albert off and closes the door behind her.* EMMA *moves to the sofa, sits on it,* R *of Daphne, and looks towards the kitchen door*)

EMMA. You'd think *I* was the unwanted visitor here, wouldn't you, the way he—(*she jerks her head towards the kitchen door*) treats me. (*Quickly and conspiratorially*) Now look, Daphne, before they come back—I'm taking Shirley up town a bit this morning. You can come, too.
DAPHNE. Oh, but . . .
EMMA. It's all right; you won't be in the way. I thought we'd give her a nice treat. We'll have a look round Marks and Spencers, and Boots, and the Co-op if we've time, and end up at Woolworths for a cup of coffee.

(ALBERT *and* CARNOUSTIE *enters from the kitchen*)

(*To Daphne. Loudly*) Sssssssh!

(*The* LADS *react to the "Sssssssh", but say nothing.* CARNOUSTIE *moves* RC. ALBERT *goes to the chair down* R *and picks up his cap*)

DAPHNE (*to Carnoustie*) Penelope all right?
CARNOUSTIE. Aye, she's fine.
EMMA. And what about that cat?
CARNOUSTIE. It's gone.
EMMA. I wouldn't trust it not to come back. It's as shifty as its owner, and that's saying something.
ALBERT (*moving up* R; *quietly*) Ready, Carnoustie?

(CARNOUSTIE *glances apprehensively at Emma, then moves to the kitchen door*)

CARNOUSTIE. Och—aye. I've just got tae get *ma* hat from next door.

ALBERT (*moving to Carnoustie*) I'll come with you.

EMMA (*rising and moving to L of the table; somewhat taken aback*) Why—what—where are you going?

ALBERT. Carnoustie and me are going for a walk.

EMMA (*in high dudgeon*) Have you asked Shirley?

ALBERT (*putting on his cap*) I'll *tell* her as we go out.

EMMA. Well—I must say . . .

ALBERT. Say what?

EMMA (*with surprised indignation*) I don't like your attitude, young man. "Tell her", indeed.

(SHIRLEY *enters from the kitchen*)

(*With satisfaction*) Ah!

(SHIRLEY *crosses to C and looks apprehensively from Albert to Emma*)

SHIRLEY. Now what?

EMMA. He says he's going for a walk.

SHIRLEY. Well—why not?

EMMA. But he hasn't asked you if he can.

SHIRLEY. Good Lord! Why should he?

EMMA (*crossing to L; with a grand gesture*) All right! All right! Do what you like. I'm finished! Through! I'll say no more.

ALBERT (*raising his voice*) Am I going, or aren't I?

EMMA (*crossing up RC and turning on Albert*) Go! Go! And do your wife out of the first bit of pleasure I expect she's been offered for months.

ALBERT (*reaching gibbering stage*) I don't know what you're . . .

EMMA (*topping him*) I'll *tell* you what I'm talking about. (*To Shirley*) I'd got it all planned; I was going to give you a nice surprise. I was going to take you—and Daphne, here—round the shops this morning, and then to Woolworths for a cup of coffee. But, of course, if you've got to stay at home just 'cos these two . . .

DAPHNE (*rising; soothingly*) Now look, Aunt Emma. We can easily settle this. Shirley can go with *you*, and I'll stay here and look after the kiddies.

EMMA (*grandly*) And why should *you* be disappointed?

CARNOUSTIE (*piping up somewhat timorously*) She'd no' be disappointed, Mrs Hornett. She doesna' care for coffee.

EMMA (*snapping loudly*) She could've 'ad an orange squash.

ALBERT (*suddenly seething*) Shirley, go and get your coat.

SHIRLEY (*crossing to L of Daphne*) What?

ALBERT. And you, too, Daphne.

DAPHNE. Now look, Albert . . .

ALBERT (*at bursting point*) For Pete's sake . . . ! Look—don't let's

have any more argument. I'm staying here with the kids—off you
go, both of you, with Ma.
    Carnoustie (*with a bleat*) And wha' aboot me?
    Albert (*almost barking*) You can go with 'em.
    Carnoustie (*yelping in horror*) Eh?
    Emma. Right! Then that's settled. There's nothing more to be
said.
    Albert (*at bursting point*) Yes, there is, just *one* thing.
    Emma (*turning; battle in her eye*) And what's that?
    Albert (*quietly*) I hope your coffee'll . . . Enjoy your coffee.
(*He strides quickly to the kitchen door*)

    (Mrs Lack *enters by the kitchen door and collides with* Albert,
*who takes her fairly roughly by the shoulders, swings her out of the way
into the room and exits to the kitchen.* Emma *looks at Carnoustie.*

    Carnoustie *turns to the door, bumps into Mrs Lack and exits to
the kitchen*)

Carnoustie (*as he goes*) Albert! Wait for me.

    (Mrs Lack *lets out a good big yelp on the collisions, and is now not
quite sure whether she is on her head or her heels*)

Mrs Lack. What 'it me? Man-'andled. That's what I was—man-
'andled.
    Emma (*sharply*) Florrie, we've no time for your wishful thinking.
Shirley, go and get your things. And bring my coat down from our
wardrobe—the biscuit one.

    (Shirley *exits to the hall*)

Mrs Lack (*moving to the easy chair and sitting*) Assault and battery,
that's what it was.
    Emma (*crossing to the sideboard and picking up her head-scarf*) Florrie,
when you've finished sitting there passing judgement . . .
    Daphne (*crossing to* l *of Mrs Lack*) Mrs Lack, will it be all right
if I pop into your house and get my things?
    Mrs Lack. 'Course you can. You know what my place is, 'ome
from 'ome.
    Emma (*muttering*) Yes, and a very long way from.
    Daphne (*moving to the kitchen door*) I won't be a minute, Aunt
Emma.
    Emma (*grumbling*) You needn't rush. I've a lot to see to yet.

    (Daphne *exits to the kitchen*)

(*She moves to* l *of Mrs Lack and puts on the scarf*) And now, Florrie,
let's get down to business.
    Mrs Lack. Business?
    Emma. How much?
    Mrs Lack. How much?
    Emma. How much for them two; putting 'em up for the night.
That's what you've come round for, isn't it?

Mrs Lack. You mean *you* want to pay for *them?*

Emma. I didn't say I *want* to, but I'm going to.

Mrs Lack (*rising; with false concern*) Oh, but, Emma, why should you? It isn't right. I mean, you didn't invite them, did you? They were wished on you.

Emma. Wished on me or not, I know my duties as an 'ostess. Bed and breakfast for two. (*Quickly and suspiciously*) They did 'ave breakfast, I 'ope?

Mrs Lack (*rather embarrassed*) Oh, yes, Emma, they did. The finest breakfast I've had in years.

Emma. H'mm! Then let's get it paid for.

Mrs Lack (*crossing to* rc; *magnanimously*) Look, Emma, I'll tell you what I'm going to do. I'm going to make a gesture. You can forget all about paying.

Emma (*suspiciously*) Well, that's very kind of you, Florrie . . .

Mrs Lack (*after the slighest pause*) But, of course—if you feel you must do *something*—well—p'raps a little present for Evadne—something small, mind, though all she seems to want at the moment is one of them high speed super bicycles. (*Quickly*) Not that I'd expect *you* to . . .

Emma (*firmly*) Bed and breakfast for two. '*Ow much?*

Mrs Lack (*crossing to the sofa and sitting; shaken*) What? (*With a little coy laugh*) Oh, dear! You do insist, don't you? Well, really, Emma, I—I don't know what to say. I mean—it isn't as if I let rooms by profession. It's ever so embarrassing.

(Emma *moves to the fireplace and takes a pound note from an ornament*)

After all—I *ask* you—what's—(*she stresses the sum a little*) a couple of pounds between friends?

Emma (*moving* c; *bitingly*) I'm glad you *ask*, 'cos you'd be told in any case; it's one pound too much.

Mrs Lack (*with no airiness*) What?

Emma. It's only the one night I'm payin' or; not their summer holidays.

Mrs Lack (*shrugging*) I'm not one to argue over money matters.

Emma. Aren't you? (*She moves to* r *of the sofa*) Well, I *am*.

Mrs Lack. But I would point out, Emma, that I've been put to a great deal of inconvenience.

Emma (*holding out the note*) One pound should cover that ample. And if it doesn't satisfy, then I'll accept that gesture of yours—and buy Evadne an ice lolly.

Mrs Lack (*quickly taking the note and putting it away*) I think we'd better not say any more about it. Personally, I was always brought up to despise commerce. (*She puts her hand to her head*) You wouldn't 'appen to 'ave an aspirin, would you? My 'ead! I didn't get a wink of sleep last night. If you'd 'eard that child of theirs howling.

Emma. Funny you should 'ear other folkses when you never 'ear your own. (*She moves to the kitchen door, opens it and calls*) Edie! (*She moves below the right end of the table)* She'll 'ave some aspirins; she's a walkin' chemist's shop, that girl.

(Edie *dashes in from the kitchen, holding a frying-pan*)

Edie (*as she enters; apprehensively*) Yes, Emma, I'm here. (*She moves to* r *of Emma*) What . . . ? (*She looks around wildly, expecting disaster*)
Emma (*irritably*) All right! All right! For the Lord's sake, it isn't the end of the world. 'Ave you any aspirins?
Edie (*eager to please*) Aspirins. Yes, Emma, I've a new bottle upstairs, but I think there's some old ones in my cupboard. I'll look. Here—'old that. (*She gives the frying-pan to Emma and crosses to the cupboard up* l) 'Ave you got an 'eadache, Emma?
Emma (*growling*) With you around not 'alf I 'aven't.

(Edie *goes into the cupboard.*
Henry *enters from the kitchen and moves to* r *of Emma*)

(*To Henry*) And here's the other 'alf of it. (*She thrusts the frying-pan into Henry's hands. Curtly*) Kitchen. (*She jerks her head towards the kitchen door*)

(Henry *exits to the kitchen.* Edie *comes out of the cupboard carrying a biscuit tin which she puts on the table*)

(*To Edie*) It isn't me that wants your aspirin. It's Florrie, here; says she's got an 'ead.

(Edie *takes various bottles, etc., from the box and peers at them*)

Mrs Lack. Ooh! I 'ave—and it's spinnin'.
Emma. I don't wonder, the scheming that goes on in it.

(Emma *crosses and exits to the hall*)

(*Off. Calling loudly*) Shirley.
Edie. I'll have to sort this out one day.

(Daphne *enters from the kitchen, carrying her coat and handbag. She puts the coat over the easy chair*)

(*Still searching*) I know they're here, somewhere.

(Daphne *crosses to* Mrs Lack, *who rises*)

Daphne (*drawing Mrs Lack down* lc) Oh, Mrs Lack.
Mrs Lack. Yes, love?
Daphne. Before Aunt Emma comes back—what do we owe you? (*She opens her handbag*)
Mrs Lack (*after a quick look towards Edie; with wide-eyed innocence*) Owe me?
Daphne (*with a touch of impatience*) For putting us up? What do we owe you?

(Mrs Lack *gives another quick look towards the occupied Edie*)

MRS LACK (*in a spurious injured voice*) Now, you're *not* going to insult me, are you?

DAPHNE (*gaping at her*) No, of course not. But you must let us pay. (*She fumbles in her bag*)

(EDIE *finds the bottle and moves below the table*)

EDIE (*peering at the unlabelled bottle*) H'mm! Yes! (*She puts the bottle on the table, with a cursory glance towards Mrs Lack, then darts to the kitchen door*) I'll get you some water.

(EDIE *exits to the kitchen*)

DAPHNE. We're very grateful to you for—er—everything, and . . .

MRS LACK (*crossing to the fireplace; grandly*) It was a gesture. And if I'm not allowed to make a gesture . . .

DAPHNE (*crossing to L of Mrs Lack; embarrassed*) Well—I don't know what to say. It's very kind of you, Mrs Lack. But you must charge us.

MRS LACK (*with acted firmness*) I couldn't. It would be on my conscience. (*Her eyes are on Daphne's bag*)

(EDIE *enters from the kitchen, carrying a cup of water*)

EDIE (*as she enters*) Here we are again. (*She goes to the table, picks up the small bottle and opens it*)

MRS LACK (*irritably*) Edie, d'y'mind? We're talking business. (*To Daphne. Quickly*) What were you saying, love?

(EDIE, *unheeding, moves to L of Daphne with the bottle and cup*)

EDIE (*holding up the bottle*) Try these, Mrs Lack; they might be aspirin. (*She thrusts the cup into Mrs Lack's hand*) How many?

(MRS LACK *is furious at Edie's interruption at a crucial moment. She scarcely hears what Edie says*)

MRS LACK (*holding out her hand; sharply*) Three.

(EDIE *shakes out some tablets into Mrs Lack's hand. MRS LACK takes the tablets and sips some water, then returns the cup to Edie*)

EDIE. There! Headache all gone, h'm?

(EDIE *goes to the table, collects the bottle top, puts it on the bottle, then slips it into her overall pocket and exits with the cup to the kitchen*)

MRS LACK. I dunno! I just daren't think what'll be the end of 'er. I expect somebody 'll kill 'er, if she doesn't kill them first. (*She puts her hand to her head. Acting hard*) Now—what were we talking about? D'y'know, it's gone clean out of my head.

DAPHNE (*taking a pound note from her bag and holding it out*) Mrs Lack—if you won't let me pay you properly—please get yourself a little present—something you'd like. I'll be very hurt if you won't.

MRS LACK. Oh, well—if you put it like that—I'm not one to

hurt a fly, really. (*She takes the note fairly quickly and slips it into her pocket*)

(DAPHNE *smiles to herself*)

(*She looks towards the hall door, obviously anxious to go*) Yes—well—I expect you've a lot to do so I'll be going. (*She moves to the kitchen door*)

(SHIRLEY, *in the hall, opens the hall door*)

EMMA (*off; calling*) Shirley! You'd better take your umbrella.
MRS LACK (*without ceremony*) Ta-ta!

(MRS LACK *exits quickly to the kitchen.* DAPHNE *picks up her coat and puts it on.*
EMMA *enters from the hall and crosses to* C.
SHIRLEY *follows her on and closes the door. Both are dressed to go out*)

SHIRLEY (*as she enters*) I haven't got an umbrella.
EMMA. Then you should 'ave. You're a married woman, now, and if that 'usband of yours can't afford to buy you one, it's a pity. (*She crosses to the kitchen door, opens it and calls*) Henry! (*She crosses to* LC) Every married woman should 'ave an umbrella.
DAPHNE. Why, Aunt Emma?
EMMA (*after a second's pause; snapping*) In case it rains. (*She crosses to the kitchen door and calls*) Henry! (*She moves* RC)

(EDIE *darts in from the kitchen*)

EDIE (*moving to* R *of Emma; breathlessly*) Yes, Emma?
EMMA (*turning and staring at her*) And since when 'ave I been married to you? I've always expected anything of you and Henry, but if you two've gone and changed sexes, then I give up. (*With a gesture of irritation*) Tell Henry I want him here; tell him I'm going.
EDIE. Yes, Emma.

(EDIE *exits to the kitchen*)

EMMA. Now, are you all ready, Daphne, 'cos we are.
DAPHNE. I'm ready.
EMMA. I suppose it *is* all right leaving those husbands of yours with the babies? They're not likely to sneak off the moment our backs are turned.
SHIRLEY (*moving* C; *irritably*) Of course they won't.
EMMA. 'Cos Edie's not to be trusted within a mile of 'em.
DAPHNE. Don't worry, Aunt Emma.

(EDIE *enters from the kitchen*)

EDIE (*moving to* R *of the table; breathlessly*) It's all right, Emma. I've told Henry you're going.
EMMA. And what's he say?
EDIE. He said, "Thank God."

D

(EDIE, *having let the words slip out, claps a hand over her mouth, and after a terrified look at Emma darts out into the kitchen*)

EMMA (*livid and practically speechless*) He—he said what? He said what?

(EMMA *charges out to the kitchen.*
      EDIE *rushes in from the kitchen, goes to the table and repacks the medicine box*)

EDIE (*wildly*) I didn't mean to tell her. It slipped out. D'you think Henry will ever forgive me?
DAPHNE. If he lives long enough.
EDIE (*whimpering*) And he was so 'appy with his ferrets.
EMMA (*off; in full spate*) Never mind what you *meant*; it's what you said that counts. How *dare* you! (*Etc., etc., ad lib*)
DAPHNE (*rushing towards the hall door*) Let's get out.
SHIRLEY (*moving towards Daphne*) Daphne, don't just leave me.

(DAPHNE *and* SHIRLEY *meet* C *and dodge each other.* SHIRLEY *loses a shoe.* EDIE *disappears behind the table. The table is covered with a large cloth which drapes over the sides, so she is hidden from view. The more the action on stage can distract from Edie's disappearance, the better.*
      DAPHNE *exits to the hall.*
      SHIRLEY, *hopping on one foot, goes to the cabinet down* R, *collects her gloves, picks up her shoe and hops off to the hall.*
      HENRY *and* EMMA *enter from the kitchen*)

EMMA (*pushing Henry in*) Get in there. If anyone had told me you could say a thing like that, Henry 'Ornett, I'd 'ave told them they could strike me dead before I'd believe it.
HENRY (*a little wearily*) Now look, Emma . . .
EMMA (*looking*) I won't look. (*Without a pause*) To send a message like that to me in front of my own daughter . . .
HENRY. I didn't send no message.
EMMA (*sweeping on*) And to send it on a day that should be one of the happiest days of my life—the day when my grandchild's to be christened; a day when we should all be 'appy, contented, and thankful for blessings received. Well, I'm not 'appy and I'm far from contented, and as for blessings received since I married you, I could count them on the little finger of one hand. (*She paces up* C *and turns*) When I think how I've been at your beck and call—(*she paces down* C) kow-towing to you—giving you the best years of my life—and then to 'ave an insult like that thrown at me. But I'll tell you this; there'll be no more becking and calling and kowing and towing. I'm finished, Henry; I'm through.
HENRY (*with the faint hope that she means it literally*) Right! (*He turns to go*)
EMMA (*almost roaring*) Henry! You'll stay where you are.

(HENRY *reluctantly stops and turns*)

If you so much as go near them—them reptiles again today . . . (*With great exasperation*) Doesn't your 'ome and what's going on in it mean anything to you? Aren't you interested in your family at all? There's your daughter—haven't spoken two words to her since she's been here, you 'aven't. You don't know *what* she's going through. (*With greater exasperation*) D'you realize that 'usband of 'ers 'asn't even bought her an umbrella? And their child—'asn't got a respectable pram to go out in; *and* he even begrudged Shirley the taxi fare from the station. You didn't know *that*, did you?

HENRY (*hardly listening*) No.

EMMA. I tell you, you don't know the half. But you're going to, my lad, you're going to know it *all*. Get this christening over and the place to ourselves again, and me and you are going to come to an understanding. (*She crosses to* L) I'm going out now.

HENRY. Thank . . . (*He remembers just in time and claps a hand over his mouth*)

EMMA (*turning and crossing to Henry*) And you know the first thing you've got to do, don't you?

HENRY. Yes.

EMMA. Then see you do it. And don't stand no nonsense from them, either. Eight pounds ten was paid, and eight pounds ten you bring back. Right?

HENRY. Right!

EMMA. Henry. And remember what I said about going out into that backyard. From now on you'll take a bit more interest in what's going on in this house—*and* in me. (*She crosses to the hall door*) I've said nothing for years, but I tell you now—I'm sick and tired of playin' second fiddle to a *ferret*.

(EMMA *exits to the hall, slamming the door behind her. A second later the front door is heard to slam.* HENRY *relaxes, moves to the easy chair and sits. He looks round the room, then automatically takes his pipe and matches from his pocket. While pressing down the tobacco already in his pipe, he unconsciously begins to hum, then sing "Home Sweet Home" quietly*)

HENRY (*singing*)
> " . . . Pleasures and palaces
> Though we may roam.
> Be it ever so humble
> There's no-o place . . ."

(HENRY *stops singing and puts his pipe into his mouth.* EDIE *puts her head out from under the table and sings the last line, her voice quavering and tearful*)

EDIE (*singing*)
> " . . . There's no-o place like Home."

HENRY (*rising*) What the . . . ?

(EDIE *rises and crosses to* L *of Henry*)

EDIE (*wildly*) I wasn't listening, Henry. I was just keeping out of the way.

HENRY (*grinning*) Till the storm blew over, eh? Well, it's blown out of the front door.

EDIE (*woefully*) And it was a storm, wasn't it? And it was all my fault. And, Henry, you will remember all Emma's told you, won't you? She's right, you know. You do spend too much time with your ferrets. Of course, I know you love them, and they love you, but . . .

HENRY. Now, for the Lord's sake, don't you start.

EDIE. I won't, Henry; I won't. (*She suddenly notices the box, etc., still on the table*) Oh! Look at all this. (*She moves to the table and begins to put the bottles back into the box*) Funny how we can neither of us do the right thing, isn't it? (*She gives a little sniff*) P'raps it's something we inherited from our ancestors. They say the sins of the fathers have got visited upon the children, don't they? (*She dries her eyes and brightens a little*) And from now on I'm going to try ever so hard to do the right thing. I . . . (*She picks up a small bottle and happens to glance at it*) Oh, *there* are the aspirins. And I was looking . . . Well, if these are the aspirin . . . (*A look of horror comes over her face. She puts the bottle on the table and quickly extracts the other bottle from her pocket*) Then *what* are . . . ? (*She rushes to Henry*) Henry!

HENRY. What now?

EDIE. Henry! What 'ave I done?

HENRY (*wearily*) Now what . . . ?

(EDIE *holds out the bottle*)

(*He takes the bottle*) Here! Where did you get these?

EDIE (*wildly*) They were in my box. I've just given three of them to Mrs Lack. I thought they were aspirins.

HENRY (*with a grin*) What was that you said just now about trying to do the right thing?

EDIE. Yes.

HENRY. Well, you've started.

EDIE. Have I?

HENRY. I've always said somebody ought to murder Florrie Lack, and you've probably done it.

EDIE (*with a shriek*) What?

HENRY (*indicating the bottle*) These are them special pills I lost; the ones you give to expecting ferrets.

EDIE *gives a horrified scream as*——

the CURTAIN *quickly falls*

SCENE 2

SCENE—*The same. Two hours later.*

When the CURTAIN *rises, the chair from* R *of the table is down* L *of it.*

Carnoustie *is seated on the chair, knitting. The pink carry-cot is on the floor beside his chair.* Albert *is seated in the easy chair and the blue carry-cot is on the floor,* l *of his chair.* Albert *is singing, very quietly, with occasional glances into his carry-cot.* Carnoustie *sings in harmony.*

Carnoustie
Albert } *(singing together)*

        "O Shenandoah,
        I long to see you.
        Away you rolling river.
        O Shenandoah,
        I long to see you.
        Away I'm bound to go
        'Cross the wide Missouri."

(They look at each other, look into their carry-cots to see if the babies are asleep, then both give the thumbs-up sign)

Carnoustie. Mine's off.
Albert *(in a whisper)* So's mine. *(He rises, picks up his carry-cot, puts it on the sofa at the right end, then tiptoes to his chair and resumes his seat)*

*(*Carnoustie *rises, picks up his carry-cot, puts it on the sofa at the left end, then tiptoes to his chair and resumes his seat. The babies cry.* Carnoustie *rises, rushes to his carry-cot and begins to sing "Shenandoah" rather wildly, though fairly quietly. He suddenly stops singing, beckons to Albert and points to Albert's carry-cot.* Albert *rises, rushes to his carry-cot and sings. The babies stop crying.* Albert *stops singing)*

Carnoustie *(smiling; quietly)* False alarm! *(He resumes his seat at the table and knits)*

*(*Albert *crosses to the fireplace)*

Albert *(after a pause)* Aaah! This is grand.
Carnoustie *(preoccupied with his knitting)* Wha' is?
Albert. This. The peace—the quiet.
Carnoustie *(agreeing vaguely)* Och—aye.
Albert *(after a pause)* You know—this is how I always used to picture married life—before I was married, of course. *(Dreamily)* Me standing with my back to the fire, the kiddie sleeping contented in his cot, and the wife sitting quietly with her knitting.

*(*Carnoustie *looks up and blinks at Albert)*

Carnoustie *(in mild protest)* A'm no' your wife.
Albert *(without looking at him; placidly)* No—but you're knitting.

*(*Carnoustie *registers puzzlement for a moment, then resumes knitting)*

(After a pause) But, somehow, it isn't like this at all. There's always something . . . *(He pauses briefly)* Mind, I'm not saying a word against Shirl. She's a wonderful wife—when she's away from here

—and I'd never find a better, but, even she—she fusses too much. (*He looks at Carnoustie*) Now, look at *you* . . .

CARNOUSTIE (*looking up*) What's wrong wi' me?

ALBERT. Nothing at all. I mean, look at you sitting there relaxed, contented with your knitting. Well, you'd never catch Shirl like that, and if I try to sit quiet for a while, she seems to get worried—suspicious—and very soon it's, "You're very silent. What's wrong?"

CARNOUSTIE (*knitting*) That's a common weakness wi' most women, Albert. And you can put it down to statistics.

ALBERT (*puzzled*) Eh?

CARNOUSTIE. In other words, to the inadequacy of the supply compared wi' the enormity of the demand.

ALBERT. What?

CARNOUSTIE. It's an established fact that there are in this worrld *six* women to every one man.

ALBERT (*grinning*) Yes—well, that leaves you Sundays free.

CARNOUSTIE. Anyway, if by sweat, blood and tears, and every trick short of Black Magic, a woman manages to snickle a man, she spends the rest of her life tormented by the knowledge that oot in the worrld there are five thwarted and ruthless females waitin' their chance to snaffle him from her. Now, after he's gone off in the morning, she spends the rest of the day prayin' he *will* come back, but convinced he won't; and by the time he *does*, every nerve in her body is dancin' an Eightsome Reel. It's all she can do to stop hersel' running up and doon the wall, screaming her heid off.

ALBERT (*crossing to* R *of Carnoustie; goggle-eyed*) Carnoustie—where—where did *you* learn all this?

CARNOUSTIE (*almost pityingly*) When you go to school in Scotland, they *teach* you something.

(ALBERT *moves to the easy chair and sits.*
EDIE *enters from the kitchen. She is in her usual state of alarmed expectancy*)

EDIE (*as she enters*) Hello! I'm back. (*She moves to* R *of the table*) Has Emma . . . ?

ALBERT
CARNOUSTIE } (*together; indicating their cots*) { (*Frantically*) Ssssh!
Ssssh, Aunt Edie!

EDIE (*panic-stricken*) What? What is it?

ALBERT (*pointing frantically to the cots; in a hoarse whisper*) They're asleep.

EDIE (*crossing below the table to the sofa*) What? (*She sees the cots*) Oh! Oh, the lambs. (*She looks into the cots. In raptures*) Bless them! (*She moves* L *of the sofa, then above it*)

(*The* LADS *watch Edie*)

(*She bends over Carnoustie's cot*) Look at him! The treasure. Isn't he handsome? The image of you, Albert.

ALBERT (*rising and crossing to* C) Aunt Edie . . .

EDIE (*unheeding; gurgling into the cot*) That's right, have a good

sleep, then you'll grow into a fine big sailor, like your daddy. (*She begins to sing, quietly but excitedly*)
                    "All the nice girls love a sailor . . ."
ALBERT (*desperately*) Aunt Edie—that's Carnoustie's baby you're looking at, and she's a *girl*.
EDIE (*flustered*) Oh! Oh! Aren't I silly?

(*The* LADS *look at each other, but say nothing*)

(*She looks into both cots*) But you'd never know, would you? They look just the same. Aren't you frightened you might get them mixed, yourselves? I mean—there's no way of telling one from another, is there?
ALBERT (*hesitantly*) Well—er—yes—there *is*.

(*The* LADS *look at each other, but say nothing*)

EDIE. Is there? How? (*She looks at the cots again*) No! don't tell me. *I* know. (*She indicates each cot in turn*) Pink for a girl; blue for a boy.

(ALBERT *collapses into the easy chair.* CARNOUSTIE *vigorously winds his wool*)

(*She crosses above the table to the kitchen door*) I must be seeing about dinner before Emma and the girls get back. (*She hesitates then moves* RC) Albert.
ALBERT. Yes, Aunt Edie?
EDIE (*desperately*) In the church—this afternoon—I want to ask a favour—can I hold baby? I *would* like to. (*She gives a little broken sob*)
ALBERT (*unhappily*) Well, I—I don't know, Aunt Edie. You see . . .
EDIE (*urgently*) I'll be able to think that if it hadn't been for my "great sorrow" it might have been my very own baby I was holding.
ALBERT. Well—er—it's a long service, I imagine—(*he indicates the cot*) and you'd find him getting very heavy, Aunt Edie. He must be getting on for nearly a stone now.
EDIE (*after a moment's thought*) I know! We've got a stone of potatoes in the kitchen. I'll just get that and have a try, shall I?

(EDIE *exits to the kitchen*)

ALBERT (*looking after Edie; scratching his head*) I dunno . . .
CARNOUSTIE. Puir Aunt Edie! (*He knits*) She's a wee bit—er . . .
ALBERT (*smiling*) She's a wee bit nothing. Aunt Edie's O.K.

(*There is a "postman's knock" at the front door*)

And if only Ma would be a bit more helpful. (*He rises and crosses to* C)

(EDIE *enters from the kitchen carrying a bag of potatoes*)

EDIE (*as she enters*) That'll be the post. I'll go.
ALBERT. No, you won't. I will. (*He smiles at the bag in Edie's arms*)

(ALBERT *exits to the hall.* EDIE, *"rocking" the bag of potatoes, moves to* R *of Carnoustie*)

EDIE (*intent on her rocking*) Funny, seeing you knitting. Is it a cardigan for little Penny-lope?
CARNOUSTIE. No, no. It's a sock—for me.
EDIE (*rocking the bag*) Why, have you lost one?

(CARNOUSTIE *looks puzzled at* EDIE, *but she is not aware of the look.*
     ALBERT *enters from the hall, carrying a letter and a newspaper in a postal wrapper*)

ALBERT (*crossing and putting the letter on the mantelpiece*) This is for Ma. (*He looks at the newspaper, rather puzzled*) And this is for me.
EDIE (*moving to* L *of Albert; still rocking the bag*) I'm doing fine, Albert. No weight at all.
ALBERT (*undoing the wrapper; vaguely*) What? Oh, good.
EDIE. Look, Albert—my baby—it's ever so light.

(EDIE *exits to the kitchen.* ALBERT *sits in the easy chair and opens the paper*)

ALBERT (*mildly puzzled*) It's last night's *Portsmouth Evening News.*
CARNOUSTIE (*vaguely*) Oh?
ALBERT. Now, who'd want to send me . . . ? (*His eyes light on the top right-hand corner of the front page, where there is a written message*) Oh! It's from our next-door neighbours. (*He reads*) "Thought you might like this. See page five. Congratulations." (*He begins to turn the pages. Puzzled*) Congratulations?
CARNOUSTIE. Ye've no' won the Pools, have ye?
ALBERT (*with a wry smile*) With eight points out of twenty-four? I should coko!
CARNOUSTIE. Then what is it?
ALBERT. Give us a chance, mate. (*He turns the pages*) Here we are. Page five—and they've marked it. (*He reads for a moment. In amazement*) Good Lord!
CARNOUSTIE. What? What is it?
ALBERT (*incredulously*) Oh, boy, oh, boy, oh, boy!
CARNOUSTIE (*rising; impatiently*) Albert . . .
ALBERT (*gaping at the paper*) Wait—*just wait* till Shirl . . .
CARNOUSTIE (*yelling*) What?
ALBERT. She'll go over the moon.
CARNOUSTIE. Albert, if ye don't tell me wha's happened . . .
ALBERT (*rising and striding down* R; *bursting with pride*) My son— *our* son—mine and Shirl's—is getting a christening mug from a royal Princess.
CARNOUSTIE (*incredulously*) No! You're joking!
ALBERT. Am I? Then take a look at that. (*He tosses the paper to Carnoustie, crosses to* R *of the sofa and leans over his cot, hardly conscious of what he is saying or doing*) Oh, boy! Oh, boy! Did you hear that,

Son? A christening mug from a Princess. Oh! (*He turns to Carnoustie. In a hoarse whisper*) D'you think I ought to wake him up and tell him?

Carnoustie (*moving* L *of the table, staring at the baby*) It's—it's astounding! I mean—an ordinary baby . . .

Albert. Ordinary? With a father like me?

Carnoustie (*grinning*) Weel, that's a matter of opeenion.

Albert (*taking the paper and striding down* R) Do you mind? I can't wait to tell Shirl—and Ma—her face when she hears . . .

Carnoustie. I've nae doot it'll make her smile. And d'you realize, Albert, if she *does* smile we'll no' recognize her.

Albert (*impatiently*) I wonder how long they'll be?

Carnoustie. It says in the paper "sending a mug". It's a pity it's no' here for the christening. Mrs Hornett would love showing it to everybody. Where will they send it, Albert? I mean—Her Royal Highness doesn't know your address, does she?

Albert (*crossing to* C) I expect what'll happen is—it'll be sent to the hospital and they'll . . . (*He puts the paper on the sofa*)

(Albert *breaks off as the front door is heard to open, followed by a mild commotion in the hall*)

Daphne (*off*) Just a minute, Shirley. I'll open the door wide.

Carnoustie. They're back. (*He tucks in the chair* L *of the table*)

Shirley (*off*) Thank you, Daphne. It's all right, Mum. I can manage.

(Daphne *enters from the hall and closes the door behind her*)

Albert. What's going on?

Daphne (*urgently*) Albert, for goodness' sake don't blow your top off. Whatever you think about it, just *say* you like it.

Carnoustie. Eh?

Daphne. And you—say nothing at all. (*She opens the door*)

(Shirley *enters from the hall, pushing a new pram.* Albert *and* Carnoustie *retreat to* R)

Shirley (*pushing the pram to* C) Make way, there. (*She crosses above the pram to* L *of Albert*)

Albert (*gaping*) Good Lord! What the . . . ? Where . . . ?

Shirley. Like it?

(Emma *enters from the hall, carrying some parcels*)

Albert (*gaping at the pram*) Yes. But—but—who—where . . . ? You *don't* mean it's *ours?*

Emma (*crossing above the pram to the table*) It is. (*She puts her parcels on the table*) And don't you try to tell me you could've got it for a penny less than thirty pounds at Portsmouth.

(Edie *enters from the kitchen, still clutching the bag of potatoes*)

EDIE (*as she enters*) What is it? (*She sees the pram*) Oh! Oh! It's a pram.

EMMA (*witheringly*) Fancy you guessing right away.

EDIE (*excitedly*) Oh, it's wonderful. I must just . . . (*She dumps the bag of potatoes into Emma's arms and rushes to the pram*)

EMMA (*looking at the bag of potatoes; annoyed*) What the . . . ?

(EDIE *crosses below the pram to* L *of it and pushes it* RC)

EDIE (*stroking the pram and almost climbing into it*) Shirley, it's beautiful! Isn't it beautiful, Albert? And look—lovely wheels—four of them. And a handle. Don't you love it, Albert?

ALBERT. I—I . . . (*He crosses down* R)

EDIE (*turning the pram and pushing it down* L) And won't you feel proud when all your shipmates see you pushing it?

EMMA (*irritably*) Edie, when you've finished crawling in and out of the pram . . .

EDIE (*rushing to* R *of Emma*) I've finished, Emma. What . . . ?

EMMA. I won't even try to guess what you were going to do with these, but you'll get 'em out of here.

EDIE. Yes, Emma. You see . . .

(EMMA *thrusts the bag at Edie and the potatoes fall out.* DAPHNE *crosses above the sofa and exits to the kitchen.* EDIE *collects the potatoes.* CARNOUSTIE *and* ALBERT *help her. They hand the potatoes to* EDIE *who puts them in the bag, but they fall out again through a hole in the bottom.* EDIE *squeaks, panic-stricken*)

EMMA (*fuming*) Look at my carpet—my clean floor . . . (*Etc., ad lib.*)

EDIE (*on her knees, scrambling after the potatoes*) It's all right, Emma; it's all right. It wasn't your fault; it was the bag. Don't worry, I'll . . .

(DAPHNE *enters from the kitchen carrying a bowl*)

DAPHNE (*giving the bowl to Edie*) All right, Aunt Edie—here's a bowl. (*She crosses above the sofa to* L)

EMMA (*moving to the sideboard*) She ought to be put away—that's the only answer—there's no other. But where could you put her? No place'd take 'er. She's too far gone.

(SHIRLEY *helps to collect the potatoes*)

CARNOUSTIE. Dinna distress yoursel', Mrs Hornett. They're soon picket up.

EDIE (*frantically*) Shirley—don't you—you'll ladder your stockings. I can manage. Albert—Carnoustie—don't you bother, either.

ALBERT (*picking up the last potato*) No bother, Aunt Edie, and that's the lot. I'll carry 'em out for you. (*He takes the bowl and moves to the kitchen door*)

(SHIRLEY *crosses down* R)

EDIE (*grabbing the bowl*) No, no. I'll take them. Just a minute, Albert.

(EDIE *runs into the kitchen, puts down the bowl and re-enters immediately*)

(*To Emma. Anxiously*) And talking of potatoes—how many shall I do for dinner, Emma?

(EMMA *turns as if about to spring on her*)

(*She realizes she has said the wrong thing and backs hurriedly to the kitchen door. Nervously*) I'll use my own judgement.

(EDIE *exits to the kitchen.* EMMA *turns away up* R, *fuming.* CARNOUSTIE *crosses and looks at the pram. There is a rather ominous silence.* ALBERT *closes the kitchen door and moves to* L *of the easy chair.* DAPHNE *sits on the right arm of the sofa*)

ALBERT (*presently; quietly*) Well—that's—that. (*He crosses to the fireplace*)

(*There is a nasty silence.* SHIRLEY *is apprehensive.* EMMA *looks significantly at Albert, then at the pram, then back to Albert. She obviously expects him to say something.* ALBERT, *however, appears to be greatly interested in one of his finger-nails*)

EMMA. Well, seeing as no-one's got anything to say, I'll just go and get rid of my things.

(EMMA *crosses to* L, *pushes the pram towards Albert and exits to the hall.* ALBERT *stops the pram* RC. SHIRLEY *moves quickly to* R *of Albert*)

SHIRLEY (*quietly but urgently*) Albert . . .
ALBERT (*indicating the pram*) I'm not going to ask whose idea it was. (*He pushes the pram* C)

(SHIRLEY *removes her coat, puts it on the chair* R *and moves to* R *of Albert*)

SHIRLEY. Now, look . . .
ALBERT (*with rising temper*) *You* didn't buy it, did you?
SHIRLEY (*crossing below Albert to* L *of him; irritably and nervously*) Of course I didn't. Mum did.

(ALBERT *gives a big sigh of exasperation and moves to the fireplace*)

ALBERT (*turning*) But why the hell did you let her?
DAPHNE. Shirley tried to stop her, Albert.
SHIRLEY (*desperately*) I *told* her you didn't want one.

(ALBERT, *for a moment, looks as though he will burst*)

ALBERT. *I* didn't want one? (*His voice rises*) Surely to God you realize the very fact that *I* didn't want one was enough to make her buy a dozen? (*He is about to shout, but manages to restrain himself and crosses to* R *of Shirley*) Did you tell her *you* didn't want one, either?

(SHIRLEY *turns to the pram and touches the handle*)

SHIRLEY (*faltering and near to tears*) I—I . . .
ALBERT. *Didn't* you?
SHIRLEY. No.
ALBERT. Well, why the hell not?

(DAPHNE *rises and removes her coat*)

DAPHNE (*calmly and reasonably*) Now look, Albert—I don't *want* to butt in on this, but I've got to.
CARNOUSTIE (*anxiously*) Now, Daphne, had ye better no' . . . ?
DAPHNE. I've got to stick up for my own sex sometimes, Scottie. (*She hands her coat to Carnoustie*)

(CARNOUSTIE *crosses to the table and puts the coat on it*)

Now, Albert—this is a lovely pram.
ALBERT (*exasperated*) I'm not saying it isn't a lovely . . .
DAPHNE (*moving to* L *of the pram; undaunted*) This—is—a—lovely —pram. (*She indicates Carnoustie and herself*) Now, *we*—(*slowly and earnestly*) we don't want one, either; they're not serviceable in flats —I *know* that, *but*—I tell you straight—if Aunt Emma had offered to buy *me* a pram like that, I'd have fallen for it just as Shirley did. *And,* what's more—I'd like to meet the young wife, with her first baby, in our position, who *wouldn't.*

(*There is complete silence for a moment, then* ALBERT *slips his arm around Shirley and draws her to him*)

ALBERT (*in a tender, but also baffled and weary voice*) I'm sorry, honey—I'm sorry.

(SHIRLEY *buries her face on his chest*)

(*He kisses the top of her head*) But it's *you* I'm thinking about. (*He looks at the pram and sighs*) Every time you take it out of the flat— and come back—there's a flight of steps to cope with. There'll you'll be—lugging your inside out when I'm not there to help—(*with a half smile*) but—if you *want* it—(*he gently lifts her chin so that she is looking at him*) if you really want it . . .

(SHIRLEY *cannot speak, but nods her head*)

(*He gives a big, baffled sigh*) O.K. There's nothing more to be said. (*He gives her a short but tender kiss*)

(SHIRLEY *puts her head on Albert's shoulder.* CARNOUSTIE *crosses to Daphne, grabs her and kisses her*)

CARNOUSTIE (*glowing*) Och! Ye're a wonderful wumman! (*He holds Daphne at arm's length then hugs her again*) An' I love ye.

(EMMA *enters from the hall, coughs, and crosses to* C. *The others break apart*)

EMMA (*looking around*) Well . . . ? (*She stands above the pram*)
ALBERT (*moving down* R; *after a slight pause*) Shirley tells me *you* bought the pram for us, Mum.
EMMA (*shortly*) I did.
ALBERT (*after a slight pause*) You shouldn't have done it.
EMMA (*shortly*) I know I shouldn't. But *I* can't help being born with a heart of gold.
ALBERT. I—I don't know what to say . . .
EMMA. You could start by saying, "Thank you."

(ALBERT *is about to speak angrily, but restrains himself, crosses below Shirley to* R *of the pram and unconsciously puts his hands on it*)

ALBERT (*quietly*) Thank you, Mum. Thank you very much. It's —it's smashing.

(*There is an awkward pause*)

SHIRLEY (*babbling anxiously*) We got it at that little shop just off the high Street—Martins. Do you know it?
ALBERT (*laconically*) No, I don't.
EMMA (*shortly*) It's a good shop.
SHIRLEY (*after a pause; desperately*) Thirty pounds, Mum paid for it.

(ALBERT, *his hands on the pram, is unable to bring himself to express thanks again*)

ALBERT (*almost inaudibly*) Smashin'.

(*There is a somewhat tense pause*)

DAPHNE (*to the rescue; bravely and too brightly*) Surprise for you, eh, Albert?
ALBERT (*without enthusiasm*) Yeh!
DAPHNE (*generally*) Nothing I like better than a really nice surprise.
SHIRLEY (*overdoing it*) Me, too. Remember last week, Daphne, when you told me . . . ?

(ALBERT *laughs quietly to himself*)

(*She turns to Albert. Alarmed*) Albert! What . . . ?

(ALBERT *crosses down* R)

EMMA (*ominously*) If there's a joke—we might as well all share it. That is, if it's fit to be heard.
ALBERT (*still laughing a little*) So you like surprises, do you, Shirl? Well, I've got one for you, haven't I, Carnoustie?
CARNOUSTIE (*blinking*) Eh?
ALBERT. The paper.

Carnoustie (*comprehending*) Och—aye—aye. (*He picks up the paper from the sofa*)

Shirley (*scared*) Albert, what is it? It isn't something awful, is it?

(Albert *crosses and stands between Shirley and Emma*)

Carnoustie. Och, no, Shirley. (*Enthusiastically*) It's no' awfu'. In fact, it's wonderful. Ye'll jump wi' joy when ye hear, and—(*to Emma; innocently*) I wouldna' be surprised if it doesna even please you, Mrs Hornett.

Emma (*turning on Carnoustie*) What?

(Carnoustie *passes the paper across Emma to Albert*)

Shirley (*quickly*) Albert, *what is it?*

Albert. Cop this, and if this doesn't make Ma burst her stays with pride, nothing will.

Emma. Eh?

Albert (*reading from the paper*) "Royal compliment for local baby. There is news today from the County Hospital, Portsmouth, which, it will be recalled, was officially opened three weeks ago by Her Royal Highness . . ."

Emma. We know all about that—get on with it.

Albert. Just a minute, Ma. (*He reads*) "We learn today from an official at the hospital that Her Royal Highness is presenting a christening mug to the first baby born in the new hospital."

Shirley. Oh—Albert, it must be our baby!

Albert (*reading*) "The child is the son of Able Seaman A. Tufnell, R.N."—that's me—"and his wife Shirley"—that's you—"of Nelson Road, Portsmouth. Baby is, we understand, to be called 'Albert' after his father. Lucky Albert Junior!"

(Shirley *is beside herself with delight and throws her arms around Albert. The following is just a babel of happy noise*)

Shirley. Oh—Albert! (*She kisses him fervently*)
Daphne (*crossing to* R *of Shirley*) Shirley—congratulations.
Shirley (*rushing to her carry-cot*) Oh, my darling baby!
Daphne. Albert! (*She kisses him*)
Albert (*beaming*) Thanks, Daphne.
Carnoustie. My congratulations, too, Shirley. (*He kisses her*)

(*They all become aware of* Emma *again, and sober up immediately on seeing her standing quite still, with a grim expression on her face*)

Shirley (*crossing to* L *of Emma; in ecstasy*) Mum, isn't it marvellous? Our son . . . (*She stops short on seeing Emma's expression*)

(*There is a pause*)

Emma (*in a quiet but ominous voice*) Is that true?
Albert. True?
Emma. What it says in the paper.

SHIRLEY (*puzzled and apprehensive*) Of course it's true, Mum. It wouldn't be *in* the paper if it wasn't. And we told you, didn't we, that the Princess had seen . . .

EMMA (*cutting in like a knife*) I'm not talking about *that*. (*She pauses briefly*) Is it true my grandson is going to be called "Albert"—after —(*with a jerk of her head towards Albert*) him?

SHIRLEY. Well—yes. I—I thought you knew.

EMMA. No—I did not.

SHIRLEY. But we've always said that—that if it was a boy we'd call him "Albert".

EMMA (*coldly*) Have we? *I* don't remember ever saying it.

ALBERT (*quietly but firmly*) Shirl and *me* have always said it, Ma. (*He pauses briefly*) And "Albert" it's going to be.

EMMA. Right! (*She goes to the kitchen door, opens it and calls, quietly but firmly*) Edie! Duster! (*She returns above the pram*)

(ALBERT *leans on the pram handle. The others, almost hypnotized, watch Emma's every movement*)

SHIRLEY (*after a pause*) Mum—what are you . . . ? Why . . . ?

(EMMA *glances coldly at* SHIRLEY *and silences her.*
EDIE *rushes in from the kitchen with a duster*)

EDIE (*moving to* R *of Emma; in her usual flutter*) I've got the duster, Emma. What is it that wants . . . ? Shall I . . . ?

(EMMA *takes the duster from Edie*)

(*Fluttering*) Oh, no, Emma, don't *you* . . . Let me . . . (*Her voice trails away as she becomes aware of an "atmosphere". After a quick look at the others, she, too, freezes into immobility*)

EMMA (*moving to Albert*) D'you mind?

ALBERT (*baffled*) Mind—what?

(EMMA *pushes Albert away from the pram.* ALBERT, *bewildered, moves* R. EDIE *goes up* C)

EMMA (*very deliberately*) They won't take this back at the shop if it's covered with greasy fingermarks. (*She rubs the handle vigorously with the duster*)

(*Near pandemonium breaks out. The following remarks come together and are more or less ad lib.*)

ALBERT. *What?*

SHIRLEY. Mum! You don't mean you're going to . . . ?

DAPHNE. Aunt Emma, you're joking!

CARNOUSTIE. Mrs Hornett, ye dinna mean to say you're . . .

EDIE. Take it back? But, Emma, you've just bought it.

(EMMA, *ignoring the others completely, dusts the body of the pram. She turns the pram and when the hubbub dies down, still dusting, she speaks to Edie but "at" Shirley and Albert*)

EMMA. Edie, when Henry gets back from Berringtons he can take this straight back to Martins in Cross Street. Thirty pounds it cost, and thirty pounds he wants. (*She gestures into the pram*) The bill's inside.

SHIRLEY (*desperately*) Mum, I can't believe you're serious.

(EMMA *straightens up from dusting, ignoring Shirley and presumably addresses Edie*)

EMMA. In the meantime—(*she hands the duster to Edie*) it isn't safe in here; too many hands and feet about for my liking, so—(*she holds the handle of the pram and circles with it so that her back is to the fireplace and the pram is pointing towards the hall door*) we'll 'ave it out in the 'all. Edie! Open that door.

(EDIE *goes to the hall door and opens it*)

(*She pushes the pram towards the hall door; raising her voice*) And don't forget to tell Henry the minute he gets back . . .

(HENRY *enters from the hall, pushing a new pram, identical with Emma's*)

HENRY (*as he enters; to Edie*) Ta. (*He pushes the pram* c) I've brought this home . . .

(*The prams almost collide* c. *There are gasps of amazement from all but* EMMA *and* HENRY)

EMMA. *Hen-ry!*

There is a split second's pause, then HENRY *turns quickly and pulls his pram off into the hall.* EMMA *follows with her pram as—*

the CURTAIN *falls*

ACT III

Scene—*The same. Early afternoon of the same day.*

When the Curtain *rises,* Henry *is sitting in the easy chair.* Edie *is sitting* R *of the table.* Daphne *is seated on the sofa, at the right end of it.* Carnoustie *is seated* L *of Daphne on the sofa.* Shirley *is standing by the hall door.* Albert *is standing behind the sofa. There is a definite atmosphere of subdued tension and expectancy.* Henry, *not quite his phlegmatic self, taps his pipe on the side of the chair. There is a pause, then there comes the sound of movement, something being put heavily on the floor upstairs.* Mrs Lack, *now smartened up for the christening, but without her hat, enters happily and normally from the kitchen.* Shirley *opens the hall door.*

Mrs Lack (*as she enters*) Hello, everybody. I just . . .

(Mrs Lack *breaks off, shaken, as the others start, turn quickly to give her an irritated glance then look upwards*)

Why—what . . . ? (*Now really shaken*) Oh, my—what is it? What . . . ?

(Edie *rises, rushes to* L *of Mrs Lack, clutches her, draws her down so that their faces are level and whispers frantically and incoherently into Mrs Lack's ear*)

No!
Edie. Yes!

(Shirley *closes the door*)

Shirley (*sharply and warningly*) Aunt Edie! (*She moves down* L)

(Henry, Daphne *and* Carnoustie *rise.* Edie *and* Mrs Lack *back to the table.* Edie *gives a little yelp and stiffens.* Mrs Lack *also stiffens in company with everyone else.*

Emma *enters briskly from the hall. She wears a two-piece costume but no hat. She surveys the assembled company with one swift look then crosses to* C)

Emma (*curtly*) Edie; my new woolly vest—I put it in the wash on Monday. Where is it?
Edie (*almost gibbering*) It's—it's on the line in the kitchen, Emma. I . . .
Emma. Get it!
Edie. I wasn't sure it was quite aired, so I . . .
Emma. Get it!

(Edie's *mouth opens, she talks soundlessly, and gesticulates vaguely*)

And if there's anything else of mine there, let me have it.

(EDIE *stumbles out to the kitchen.* EMMA *crosses to the sideboard, takes her handbag and a Post Office Savings book from the drawer and puts the book in her bag. She goes to the mantelpiece, takes some money from a vase and puts the money in her bag and moves* C. *She returns to the mantelpiece, takes a photograph from the top shelf, moves* C *and waits for Edie, tapping her foot. Her movements are watched in silence by the others.*

EDIE *flounders in from the kitchen, carrying one or two articles of underwear. She moves to* R *of Emma, goggling at her, thrusts the garments into her arms then retreats to* R *of the table.* EMMA *quickly checks each article then moves swiftly to the hall door. She is about to exit, changes her mind and turns to throw a remark at Mrs Lack)*

Florrie! (*She points*) That old blue dress of yours—it's dyed very nicely.

(EMMA *exits to the hall. Everyone relaxes bodily, but there is still an atmosphere of anxiety.* HENRY, DAPHNE *and* CARNOUSTIE *resume their seats.* SHIRLEY *moves to Albert.* MRS LACK, *however, is not anxious, merely indignant at Emma's remark)*

EDIE (*tremulously*) Emma's going to leave home.

MRS LACK (*moving down* C; *plaintively indignant*) It isn't me old blue at all! I only bought this last week.

EDIE (*rushing to* L *of Mrs Lack; anxious to console her*) Emma didn't really mean it—it's just that it *looks* old.

MRS LACK (*indignantly*) Well! Let me tell you, Edie, this dress cost me . . .

SHIRLEY (*desperately and impatiently*) Mrs Lack—*please*. We're all desperately worried.

(ALBERT *moves up* R *of the sofa)*

MRS LACK (*crossing to the fireplace; somewhat hoity-toity*) Yes, of course, you must be. I can understand that. And I wouldn't have come in at all just now, but I wanted to ask Edie about them aspirins she gave me.

EDIE (*moving to* L *of the easy chair; alarmed*) Why, Mrs Lack? Have they . . . ? They haven't . . . ?

MRS LACK. Yes, Edie. (*With enthusiasm*) They're wonderful. They don't just clear your 'ead, they—(*she crosses to* RC) they *do* something to you. They make you feel—ooh, I dunno—*different*, if you know what I mean. (*She preens herself a little)*

(HENRY *looks at Mrs Lack for a moment without comment, then turns away)*

(*Aware of this*) I was feelin' ever so gay and light-'earted—till I came in here.

ALBERT (*pacing down* C) Well, why don't you go out again? (*He paces up* C)

(SHIRLEY *moves* C)

SHIRLEY (*suddenly snapping; with a touch of hysteria in her voice*) Albert, will you for goodness' sake stop walking up and down like that. My nerves won't stand it.

(ALBERT *stops abruptly. He is about to snap back at Shirley, but refrains, crosses and sits in the chair down* R)

DAPHNE (*rising and moving* R *of the sofa*) Come and sit down, Shirley. You . . .

SHIRLEY (*almost shouting*) I don't want to sit down. (*She crosses and sits on the sofa, at the right end of it*)

(MRS LACK *crosses to the fireplace*)

EDIE (*sitting* R *of the table; tremulously*) Shirley, love . . .

SHIRLEY. What are we going to do? We can't let Mum just walk out of the house like this. We've got to stop her.

DAPHNE (*quietly*) She hasn't gone yet.

SHIRLEY. But she's going. She's told us she is. (*Witheringly*) You don't think she's *joking*, do you?

DAPHNE. I wouldn't know what goes on in Aunt Emma's mind. We're not tuned in to the same wave-length.

MRS LACK (*with great relish*) Oh, she's going all right.

(EDIE *gives a strangled wail.* SHIRLEY *rises*)

I mean—look at the way she took that wedding photograph from the mantelpiece. Gruesome, wasn't it?

SHIRLEY (*moving below the table; impatiently*) Mum isn't going for good, Mrs Lack.

MRS LACK. Has she *told* you she isn't?

SHIRLEY (*the doubt now in her mind*) No, of course, she hasn't, but —she wouldn't—she couldn't. Oh, my . . . ! (*She crosses to* L *of Henry*) Dad, you don't think . . . ?

MRS LACK. I wouldn't be too sure, Shirley love. Once the cage door is open and the bird flies out . . .

HENRY (*almost shouting*) Emma isn't a bloody linnet.

EDIE (*rising; wailing*) Don't, Henry! Don't swear and don't get excited. We know she isn't a bloody linnet. (*She realizes what she has said and collapses in grief again. Loudly and hysterically*) It's all my fault. Emma wouldn't be leaving home if it hadn't been for me. Oh, Emma, I don't know how you've put up with me all these years. *I* couldn't have done. It's me that's broken up your home, Henry. Why don't you strike me dead at your feet?

HENRY (*quietly*) It's on the agenda.

EDIE (*dramatically*) But I won't let it happen. Emma shan't go. I will. Don't tell her I'm going, Henry, then when she comes down and finds I've gone it'll be a heavenly surprise.

(EDIE *exits brokenly to the kitchen.* DAPHNE *sits* R *of Carnoustie on the sofa*)

MRS LACK (*goggling*) Well, I must say . . .

HENRY (*fuming*) You do, and I won't be responsible for what 'appens.

SHIRLEY. Mrs Lack, please—go to her. See if you can calm her down. Make her a cup of tea or—or something.

MRS LACK (*moving to the kitchen door*) Right! I know, I'll get her to take half a dozen of them pills of hers.

(MRS LACK *exits to the kitchen.* HENRY *rises and moves to the fireplace*)

HENRY (*fumbling with his pipe; fuming*) Women! Women! If we had a Government any good at all, they'd bring in a law against 'em—specially Florrie Lack. (*He jabs his pipe in his mouth but it will not "draw"*)

SHIRLEY (*moving to L of Henry; angrily*) Well, at least Mrs Lack is capable of doing *something*, which is more than *you* are, apparently.

HENRY (*trying to control himself*) Now don't you start . . . (*Loudly*) Blast this pipe!

SHIRLEY. What have you done to stop Mum clearing out?

HENRY (*searching on the mantelpiece for a pipe cleaner*) Not a damn thing, and I'm not going to.

SHIRLEY. But, Dad, you don't want Mum to go.

HENRY. If she wants to go, I can't stop her.

ALBERT. *Why* can't you?

HENRY (*almost shouting*) Because . . . (*He hesitates, then blusters*) This damn thing—stopped up—I'll have to go out to the shed—find a bit of wire.

(HENRY *exits to the kitchen*)

EDIE (*off; wailing*) Hen-ry!
HENRY (*off; roaring*) Shurrup!

(ALBERT *rises, goes to the sideboard, looks on it, and runs his hand desperately through his hair*)

ALBERT. Where's my cap? (*He looks wildly around*)
SHIRLEY (*moving to L of Albert*) Your cap? Albert, you're not going out?

ALBERT (*crossing to C*) I've got to, Shirl; just for a while, otherwise I shall go completely off my nut.

(SHIRLEY *follows Albert to C*)

I can stand just so much of your mother and this house, and I've had my fill of both. (*Irritably*) Why can't I *never* find my hat? (*He spins around and bumps into Shirley*) Sorry, honey. (*He moves to L of the table and searches around, under the chairs, etc.*)

SHIRLEY (*following Albert*) But, Albert—the christening! If Mum isn't coming—what are we going to do about the christening?

(ALBERT *moves below the sofa and looks on it.* SHIRLEY *follows to R of the sofa*)

ALBERT. I'll tell you—when I've found my hat.

SHIRLEY (*with a trace of irritation*) When you've . . . ?

ALBERT. Yes. 'Cause the moment I tell you, I want to be ready to run for it. (*He crosses to* L *of the sofa and looks behind it*)

SHIRLEY (*alarmed*) Albert, don't do anything foolish.

ALBERT (*going on his knees behind the sofa and feeling under it; his voice a mumble*) Just you wait till . . .

CARNOUSTIE (*suddenly leaping to his feet; with a wild yelp of surprise*) Aaaah!

(*There is a howl of pain from* ALBERT)

DAPHNE (*gaping at Carnoustie*) What on earth . . . ?

SHIRLEY (*overlapping*) Carnoustie!

CARNOUSTIE (*clutching his ankle*) A ferret! (*He moves down* L *of the sofa*)

DAPHNE. *What?* (*She quickly kneels on the sofa*)

(SHIRLEY *moves down* C)

CARNOUSTIE. A bluidy ferret! (*He points under the sofa*) Under there! A'm telling ye.

(ALBERT *rises to his feet behind the sofa, clutching his hand*)

ALBERT (*in agony*) My hand!

CARNOUSTIE (*surprised*) Did it get you, too, Albert?

ALBERT (*with ferocity*) The only thing that got me, you clot, was your big clumping foot.

CARNOUSTIE. It was your hand, and I thought it was one of Pop's ferrets. (*Interested*) Now why should I think it was a ferret?

ALBERT. I'll tell you why, Son. Because this house is having the same effect on you as it is on me. It's sending us both up the wall. (*Suddenly, as if a new thought*) Where's my hat? (*He moves to the window*)

(SHIRLEY *moves to* L *of the table.*
EDIE *enters from the kitchen with her coat and beret*)

EDIE (*over her shoulder into the kitchen; with suppressed excitement*) Yes, Mrs Lack. I'll go and ask her. (*She closes the door, stands at it for a moment, then moves conspiratorially down* RC) Ssssh!

ALBERT (*puzzled*) Eh?

EDIE (*loudly*) Sssssssh! Emma—where is she? Is she still upstairs?

(ALBERT *moves to* L *of the easy chair.* SHIRLEY *moves to* L *of Edie*)

DAPHNE. For all we know, she is. Why, Aunt Edie? (*She rises*)

EDIE (*after much mysterious gesturing*) Mrs Lack thinks she's got me to see sense, but she hasn't. I won't. She thinks I'm going to ask Emma if she'd like a cup of tea—but I'm not.

ALBERT (*blankly*) I don't blame you.

EDIE (*wildly but contritely*) Oh, I'd like her to have a cup of tea, but—(*in a broken voice*) I don't want her to see me—(*she sobs*) not till after I've gone.

SHIRLEY. Aunt Edie, this is nonsense. You're not going. You mustn't.

EDIE (*weeping*) I must. I must. It's the only way to bring happiness back into this house. (*She hands her coat and beret to Daphne*) Here—'old that. (*She moves up* R *and indicates the cupboard over the kitchen door*) Give me a hand up here—my suitcase is in that cupboard. Get the table. (*She draws out the chair* R *of the table*)

(CARNOUSTIE *crosses and helps* EDIE *to move the table to the kitchen door.* ALBERT *takes the chair and puts it on the table.* DAPHNE *fetches the chair from* R *of the window and puts it below the table.* EDIE, *helped by* CARNOUSTIE, *steps on to the chair, then on to the table and then on to the chair on the table.* SHIRLEY *is above the easy chair.* ALBERT *is* R *of the table.* CARNOUSTIE *is* L *of the table.* DAPHNE *moves to* L *of Carnoustie*)

SHIRLEY. But where will you go?

(EDIE *opens the cupboard and various vacuum cleaner tubes, etc., fall out. She takes a suitcase from the cupboard and climbs to the floor*)

EDIE. What does it matter, now? My little world has collapsed around me. (*She crosses to* LC *and opens the case, and various articles of clothing fall out. Wildly*) You see? You see? It's Fate. I'm a marked woman! Fate has put its finger on me. Whatever I do—wherever I go, I leave a trail of destruction behind me. (*Wildly*) Oh, I'll pick it all up. (*She bundles the clothing into the case*) I've destroyed Henry and Emma's happiness. (*To Shirley*) Now I'm destroying yours.

(DAPHNE *goes to Edie and hands her the coat and beret*)

But when I've gone—perhaps the angel of peace will come in my place—and talk to Emma. If she gives him the chance.

(EDIE *exits to the hall.* ALBERT, DAPHNE, CARNOUSTIE *and* SHIRLEY, *during the following speeches, replace the tubes, etc., in the cupboard, and move the table and chairs into their original positions*)

DAPHNE. Good Lord! You don't think she means it, do you? You don't think she will go, as well?

SHIRLEY. Of course she won't. It's not *her* I'm worried about—It's Mum. If she goes it'll be awful.

ALBERT (*grimly*) It will; for whoever she goes to.

SHIRLEY (*desperately*) But what about the christening? I'll feel terrible if Mum isn't there. Whatever will it look like?

(*When the room is tidy,* ALBERT *perches on the table;* CARNOUSTIE *stands up* R *of the sofa;* DAPHNE *sits on the right arm of the sofa and* SHIRLEY *sits* R *of the table*)

ALBERT. A damn sight prettier than if she *was*.

SHIRLEY (*sharply*) Albert, will you please remember you're talking about my mother?

ALBERT (*raising his voice*) I don't want any reminding.

CARNOUSTIE (*quietly*) If I might put in a word—you're tackling this thing from the wrong angle.

ALBERT. What thing?

CARNOUSTIE. Mrs Hornett.

ALBERT. Oh!

SHIRLEY (*rounding on Carnoustie*) *What* do you mean?

CARNOUSTIE (*hastily*) I mean—her proposed departure into outer space. You're letting her see you're worried aboot it.

ALBERT. I'm not worried.

CARNOUSTIE. No, but you look it, and she *enjoyed* seeing you look that way. You just played into her hands. But if you could make her feel you didna' care a damn whether she went or no'—she'd change her ideas, I'm thinking.

DAPHNE. And how do you propose we do it?

(EMMA *sweeps in from the hall.* CARNOUSTIE *goes off into what he imagines to be natural and hearty laughter.*
EMMA *glares at Carnoustie, crosses and exits to the kitchen*)

CARNOUSTIE. There you are! (*Excitedly*) You see? That's a beginning. Now, if you could all just . . .

ALBERT (*laughing*) You think she was taken in by *that?* (*He laughs loudly*) Blimey! What a hope!

CARNOUSTIE (*indignantly*) She heard me laughing, didn't she?

ALBERT (*laughing*) Laughing? Sounded more like a death-rattle.

CARNOUSTIE. Well, if you think you can do any better . . .

(EMMA *enters from the kitchen, carrying a cup of tea.* CARNOUSTIE *laughs.* ALBERT *roars with laughter at Carnoustie.* DAPHNE *and* SHIRLEY *laugh quite genuinely at Carnoustie.* ALBERT *rises. Everyone is laughing.* EMMA *stops abruptly down* RC)

ALBERT (*almost doubled*) Stop it, Carnoustie. I can't stand it! (*Without realizing it, he has moved close to Emma. He looks at her blankly for a moment then bursts into genuine laughter again. He addresses Emma, not rudely, but "helplessly"*) Hello, Ma. Want any help with the packing?

(EMMA, *looking as if she would burst, sweeps out to the hall.* ALBERT *crosses to* L *of the sofa*)

CARNOUSTIE (*very excitedly*) Y'see? Y'see? That's caught her where it hurts the most. Och, it was a stroke of genius, Albert. "Do you want any help with the packing?" Just you wait! In a wee while she'll be doon, saying she's no' going at all.

(EMMA *enters from the hall. The others, caught unawares, give a start*)

EMMA (*sharply*) Shirley!

SHIRLEY (*rising; apprehensively*) Yes, Mum?

EMMA. Find your father. Tell him I've changed my mind.

SHIRLEY (*delighted*) Oh, Mum—I'm so glad.

EMMA (*firmly*) I'm not going on the train at three o'clock.

CARNOUSTIE (*beaming with pride*) I *thocht* maybe you wouldna' be.
EMMA. I'm going on the bus at half past two.

(EMMA *exits to the hall.* SHIRLEY *resumes her seat. They all gape after Emma*)

ALBERT (*crossing above the sofa to* L *of Carnoustie*) Got any more bright ideas, Son? No? Not any of you? (*Business-like*) Right! Then p'raps you won't mind if *I* make a suggestion. (*He consults his watch. To Shirley and Daphne*) It's nearly two o'clock. How long will it take you to get the bags packed and the kids ready to travel?
SHIRLEY. Why, what are you . . . ?
ALBERT. What I'm suggesting is, that the four—the six of us—get ourselves out of here and back to Portsmouth as soon as possible.
DAPHNE. Suits me. But what about . . . ?
SHIRLEY (*overlapping*) What about the christening?
ALBERT. Forget it.
SHIRLEY (*irritably*) Albert, for goodness' sake! You can't just say "Forget it" like that. It's all arranged.

(ALBERT *gives a big sigh and crosses to* R *of Shirley*)

ALBERT (*patiently*) Now listen, Shirl. I'm not trying to be awkward, but—a christening's supposed to be a reasonably happy event, a sort of "knees up", isn't it? Now—God knows whether your mother *would* turn up or not—so—either way you look at it, it seems like being a bit of a carve-up.

(SHIRLEY *nods*)

(*He puts his arms round Shirley*) Let's go home, honey. The christening's cancelled—so what? We'll have the job done at Portsmouth. I'll ask the chaplain to do it. (*He grins*) Full naval honours and a royal salute, with that christening cup, eh? (*He pauses*) How about it?
SHIRLEY (*after a pause; quietly*) What time do you say it is?
ALBERT. About two o'clock.
SHIRLEY. He shouldn't be wakened for another ten minutes or so, but—(*she rises and pushes her chair into the table*) it'll give me time to pack.
ALBERT. Good for you, Shirl. (*He kisses her*)

(SHIRLEY *crosses to the hall door.* ALBERT *sits in the easy chair*)

DAPHNE (*rising*) Oh, Shirley—our things are over at Mrs Lack's. As soon as I've packed I'll come up and see to Penelope. Don't you bother. (*She crosses to the kitchen door*)

(SHIRLEY *exits to the hall*)

(*To Carnoustie*) You'd better come and give me a hand.
CARNOUSTIE. A'm no' a packer.
DAPHNE. No, but you're a carrier. (*She moves above the table*) Oh, and by the way——

CARNOUSTIE. What?
DAPHNE. —you owe me a pound; Mrs Lack; I settled with her this morning. She didn't want to take it—she said, but . . .
CARNOUSTIE (*hooting*) *You?* You gave her a pound?
DAPHNE. I did.
CARNOUSTIE (*with a howl of misery*) Ma God! So did I.
DAPHNE. *What?*
CARNOUSTIE. Oot in the garden. Said she'd take it, but only as a gesture.
DAPHNE (*almost speechless*) She said . . . And you . . . Ooh! *Two* pounds for . . . And I bought the breakfast! Ooh! That woman! I'll—I'll tear her to pieces. I'll . . . (*She opens the kitchen door, steps just inside, gives a little start, then speaks in almost honeyed tones*) Oh! Hello, Mrs Lack. (*Quite pleasantly*) D'you mind if I pop over to your place and . . .
MRS LACK (*off; pleasantly*) Do whatever you want to, love.
DAPHNE. Thank you, dear.

(DAPHNE *exits to the kitchen.* CARNOUSTIE *goes to the kitchen door, closes it, then moves above the table*)

CARNOUSTIE (*indignantly*) Och! The two-facedness of women! Did y' hear, Albert?
ALBERT (*grinning*) I heard.
CARNOUSTIE (*babbling*) I wouldna' have believed it of Daphne. After being robbed of a whole pound—*twenty* shillings. If the day ever comes when I say one thing and mean another, I hope I may be struck down, and . . .

(MRS LACK *enters from the kitchen and moves above the easy chair*)

(*He moves to* L *of Mrs Lack*) I—I . . . (*With a rather wan smile*) Nice day, Mrs Lack.

(CARNOUSTIE *gives a start, looks heavenwards then exits quickly to the kitchen, puzzled, then closes the door*)

MRS LACK (*amiably*) Funny people, Scotties, aren't they?
ALBERT. Are they?
MRS LACK. Always seem as if they're saying one thing—and meaning another. (*She moves* C) Like a cup of tea?
ALBERT (*rising and crossing to the sofa*) No, thanks. (*He sits on the sofa, at the right end of it*)
MRS LACK. There's plenty in the pot.

(ALBERT *shakes his head*)

(*She moves to the fireplace*) Oh, well, I don't blame *you*, in the circumstances. Mind you, it's *Mr* Hornett my heart goes out to. 'Course, she may not stay away for long.
ALBERT. Then my heart goes out to him, too.

(HENRY *enters from the kitchen and moves to the easy chair*)

Mrs Lack. Oh, Mr Hornett—poor Mr Hornett.

(Mrs Lack *helps* Henry *to sit in the easy chair.* Henry *glares at her*)

Just you sit down there and make yourself cosy and I'll get you a nice cup of tea.

(Mrs Lack *exits to the kitchen*)

Henry. What's the matter with Lolita?
Albert (*after a slight pause*) Pop, Ma's changed her mind, she says.
Henry (*quickly, but without expression*) You mean she isn't going?
Albert (*after a look at Henry*) No. She's going at half past two—by bus—instead of three.
Henry (*non-committally*) I see.
Albert (*after a slight pause*) And Shirl and me and the others are going back to Portsmouth, straight away.
Henry. But what about the christening?
Albert. We've talked it over and decided it's best to postpone it.
Henry. I see.
Albert (*rising and moving* c) You don't give much away, do you?
Henry. What d'you mean?
Albert (*moving to* l *of Henry*) I'd like to know what's going through your mind.
Henry. It might surprise you.
Albert. I believe you're—upset—'cos Ma's going; are you?
Henry. To tell you the truth, Son, I don't know. (*Quickly*) Oh, I know I've often said I'd give anything for the chance to be on my own for a bit—but—now it looks like happening . . . Nearly thirty years we've been married—and you can learn to put up with a hell of a lot in thirty years.
Albert (*moving* c; *muttering*) Thirty years of . . . Blimey!
Henry (*quickly*) Oh, I know, I know. Thirty years of Ma doesn't seem possible to you, but—right now—a few days without her doesn't seem possible to *me*. We've never been separated—not for a single night—in all our married life—and I'm scared.
Albert (*moving to* l *of Henry*) Scared you'll be unhappy when she's away, you mean?
Henry (*with a burst*) You damn young fool! I don't mean that at all.
Albert (*gaping*) Then what . . . ?
Henry (*with emphasis*) I'm scared I'll be so happy, I won't be able to stand it when she comes back.
Albert (*goggling at him*) What? (*Baffled, he strikes his forehead several times with the palm of his hand and crosses to* c)

(Mrs Lack *enters from the kitchen with a cup of tea*)

Watch it, Pop—here's Lolita again. I'll just slip up and see if Shirl's nearly packed. We'll need a taxi—four of us—and the kids.

(ALBERT *exits to the hall.* MRS LACK *moves to* L *of Henry and gapes after Albert*)

MRS LACK. Packed? Don't say they're going, as well. What about the christening?
HENRY (*gruffly*) Nothing about the christening; it's off, seemingly.
MRS LACK (*handing the tea to Henry; with sorrowful indignation*) Well, I think that's the last straw; even the child has to be done out of its natural rights. All I can say is—I mean no disrespect, *but*—I wouldn't like to have Emma's conscience at this moment.

(HENRY *sips his tea*)

HENRY. Did *you* make this tea?
MRS LACK (*moving* RC) I did.
HENRY (*putting the cup of tea in the grate; quietly*) You can't 'ave a conscience at all.
MRS LACK (*after a slight pause*) Well, this *is* a nice how-d'you-do, isn't it? You left all on your own, eh?

(HENRY *grunts*)

Well, there's nothing else for it.

(HENRY *looks at her*)

It looks as if I'm going to have a man on my hands again. It's a few years now since my late husband passed on.
HENRY (*apprehensively*) What are you suggesting?
MRS LACK. Well, if Emma's leaving you—you'll have to have *somebody*, won't you?
HENRY (*burbling*) Eh?
MRS LACK (*sweeping on happily*) Well, I may not be your "dearest", but I'm your "nearest", aren't I? Your next-door neighbour, I mean. And after all, what's a next-door neighbour for; specially when she's a woman.
HENRY (*with feeble severity*) Mrs Lack, I think this conversation's gettin' out of 'and.

(*There is a slight pause.* MRS LACK *moves* RC)

MRS LACK (*frigidly*) Mr Hornett—I'm talking about someone to cook your meals for you.
HENRY (*embarrassed*) Oh—I—er—yes—I—er—I see your trend.
MRS LACK (*shocked*) You wasn't thinking . . .
HENRY (*with assumed airiness*) No, no, no, no, no.
MRS LACK. 'Cos if you was . . . Ooooh! You aren't 'alf barking up the wrong tree. (*She crosses to the fireplace*) No, I'm simply offering to come in and get your meals for you.
HENRY (*hastily*) I wouldn't dream of troubling you.
MRS LACK (*as an idea occurs to her*) Yes, why not?

HENRY (*apprehensively*) Why not what?

MRS LACK. No point in cooking twice over. Me and Evadne could pop over and have our meals in here. Company for you, and a change for Evadne. (*Sweeping on*) Now, we'll have to think up some nice surprises for you, won't we? Do you like roly-poly puddings?

HENRY (*hastily removing his pipe from his mouth*) Cor!

MRS LACK. Jam ones, I mean. Evadne does; she practically lives on them.

HENRY (*desperately*) Now look, Mrs Lack . . .

MRS LACK. I know, I know. You'd rather not discuss it. You're the same as all men; like your meals to be a surprise. Well, you can leave it to me. They will be. (*She crosses to L of Henry*) You won't know what's happened to you, will you, Mr 'Ornett; being master in your own house for the first time, as you might say? Being able to do what you like—where you like—breathe when you want to. (*She crosses to C*) My! You will 'ave a beano.

(HENRY *rises slowly and moves up* RC, *his mind very occupied*)

HENRY. Thank you very much, Mrs Lack.

MRS LACK. Eh?

HENRY. For putting ideas into my head.

MRS LACK (*puzzled*) You mean the roly-poly pudding?

HENRY (*moving to the kitchen door; to himself*) What I like—where I like . . .

(HENRY *exits to the kitchen*)

MRS LACK. Now what's the matter with him? Must be second childhood. (*She looks critically around for a moment, then goes to the sideboard, picks up an ornament, moves to the fireplace, takes up an ornament from the mantelpiece and replaces it by the one from the sideboard*) I never did understand Emma's taste in china—shocking. (*She crosses to* L *with the ornament from the mantelpiece*)

(EMMA *enters from the hall. She wears her hat*)

(*With her back to the hall door*) Now—what shall I do with this? (*She looks around and sees Emma*) Ooh!

(EMMA *sees the ornament in Mrs Lack's hand, takes it from her and crosses to the fireplace*)

EMMA. Very nice, I'm sure, Florrie, but it isn't for sale.

MRS LACK. I like your 'at.

(EMMA, *about to replace the ornament on the mantelpiece, sees the one transferred by Mrs Lack*)

EMMA. You might let me get out of the house before you begin to play Snakes and Ladders with my ornaments. (*She returns the ornaments to their original places*) Where's Henry?

MRS LACK. He just popped out.

Emma. I've got to give him a lot of instructions, so it's time he popped in again. And, Florrie, p'raps you won't mind popping home. (*She moves to* R *of the table*)
Mrs Lack (*moving to* L *of the table; airily*) No—I don't mind.
Emma (*pointedly*) It'll make a change, won't it?

(Henry, *whistling happily, enters from the kitchen carrying a roll of wire-netting under one arm, and a tool-box under the other*)

(*She turns*) What . . . ? (*Sharply*) Henry!

(Henry *drops the netting on the floor below the easy chair and hands Emma the tool-box*)

Henry. Pop that down.
Emma (*stunned*) What?
Henry (*indicating the table*) On there.

(Henry *exits to the kitchen*)

Emma (*goggling at the box*) Well! Did you hear?
Mrs Lack (*very happily*) Yes. He said, "Pop it on there."

(Mrs Lack *indicates the table then exits to the kitchen.* Emma, *dazed, puts the box on the table and moves* C.
Henry *enters from the kitchen, his head lost to sight as he carries Edie's wooden cradle. He puts the cradle on the table*)

Emma (*goggling*) What's going on here? I want to know. Henry—what is it?
Henry (*easily*) Oh—you still 'ere. Little job. Bit nippy outside. 'Ad an idea you'd gone. (*He goes on his knees and lays out the wire-netting*)
Emma (*moving* RC; *reproachfully*) Henry, you didn't think I'd go without saying good-bye?
Henry (*rising, picking up the wire and moving to the table*) Albert doesn't want this after all. (*He indicates the cradle*)
Emma. What?
Henry. So I'm turning it into a playroom for Rosie's young 'uns. 'Course, I wouldn't've brought it in here to do if I'd known you were still 'anging around.
Emma (*almost speechless*) 'Anging . . . ?
Henry. I mean, I'd've waited before starting to mess the place up. (*Reassuringly*) But you are going soon, aren't you?
Emma. What you'll do, is—listen to what I've got to say.
Henry (*straightening the wire*) But, Emma, when you told us you were going, you said you'd said your last word.
Emma (*rattled*) Yes—well—I've thought of a few more.

(Henry *has straightened the wire and moves to the tool-box*)

Henry (*with a patient sigh*) I see.
Emma (*firmly*) Henry, I know I'm leaving you, but I haven't made up my mind whether it's for good or not.

HENRY. Oh, it *is*.

EMMA. It's you that's driven me to it—you realize that, don't you? You and everyone else. I've got to get away, Henry; I've *got* to.

HENRY (*amiably*) Oh—all right. Off you pop.

EMMA (*pressing on*) Even my own daughter defying me into the bargain.

HENRY. But, Emma, she 'as a right to call her own child what she likes.

EMMA. I'm saying no more about it. I'm going, and that's that. (*She crosses to* L)

HENRY (*vaguely*) Good.

(EMMA *stops, reacts, turns and crosses to* L *of the table*)

EMMA. But before I go—I'd just like to know you'll be all right.

HENRY. That's nice of you, Emma. (*He takes sundry tools from the box*)

EMMA. Well, I'm human, aren't I?

HENRY (*after a slight pause; kindly*) Now, look, Emma, we won't start an argument just when you're going.

EMMA. Besides, I'm not having the whole world say I went off like a will-o'-the-wisp, without a thought of the wreck I was leaving behind.

(HENRY *looks up*)

I know what they're *like* in the street. I want everything straightened out before I go. So first—you'd better see the milkman in the morning and tell him to deliver half a pint less each day from now on. I can't see you getting two pints of milk a day down you, can you?

HENRY. No.

EMMA. Now—as to food. You'll find plenty in the larder to see you over the next day or two. And do you know how to cook yourself a chop?

HENRY. T', t', t'. (*He makes gentle "silencing" gestures with one hand*)

EMMA. It's easy enough. All you have to do is . . . (*She becomes aware of Henry's gestures and repeats herself, her voice dying away*) All you have to do is . . . (*Loudly and sharply*) What are you waving at me for?

HENRY. Just trying to tell you to save your breath. There's nothing for you to worry about, it's all buttoned up.

EMMA. What is?

HENRY. My domestic arrangements.

EMMA. How can they be? I 'aven't—buttoned 'em, yet.

HENRY. You 'aven't, no. But you know the old saying—"There's always somebody just around the corner . . ."

EMMA (*gaping; unbelievingly*) The old saying? (*Ominously*) Henry Hornett, who is there just around your corner?

HENRY (*busy with the wire-netting*) Florrie Lack.

EMMA (*with a yelp*) What?

HENRY. But only in a—a nice way, you understand. At least, I *think* . . .

EMMA. What are you trying to tell me?

HENRY. She's going to come in and get my meals ready.

EMMA (*with a yelp*) She's coming in here?

HENRY. And her and Evadne are going to come and help me eat 'em.

EMMA (*babbling*) Eat 'em!

HENRY. Company like. And 'praps they'll do a bit of dusting.

(EMMA *paces to the window and back*)

EMMA (*rampaging*) *Dusting?* That woman's never had a duster in her hand for the last twenty years. She's forgotten what they're used for. Not that one would be any use in her house; you'd need a pick-axe. And you're going to let her run free in here—her and that bladder of a child of hers that's likely to burst at any minute and most likely do it in my kitchen just for spite?

HENRY. Only at meal times.

EMMA (*tapping her foot*) *Meal* times? And what sort of meals are you going to get from Florrie Lack?

HENRY (*murmuring*) Roly-poly puddings . . .

EMMA (*at bursting point*) Roly-poly . . . ? If she ever made any roly-poly puddings they'd be used to build bomb-proof shelters. (*Stronger*) Have you ever seen the inside of her oven? I'd be ashamed to cook a skunk in it. And you were going to let her come in here and use my . . . Right! (*She pauses for a moment then removes her coat and hat in almost one movement and throws them on to the sofa. The hat falls to the floor. She is now very much her old self. She points to the cradle*) *That— out!*

HENRY. Eh?

EMMA (*grabbing the tools and throwing them into the box*) Out! (*She snatches the wire-cutters from Henry*) And your this! (*She hurls them into the box and grabs the pliers*) And your that! (*She crosses to* L) I'm going up to unpack. If this table isn't cleared and everything outside by the time I come down . . .

HENRY. But, Emma—what about the two-thirty bus?

EMMA. You can put the two-thirty bus——

(HENRY *looks up, startled*)

—*out of your mind.*

(EMMA *sweeps out to the hall, slamming the door behind her.* HENRY *looks after her for a moment and sighs*)

HENRY. Well—for better or wuss, that's shut the cage door well and ruddy truly. (*He picks up the cradle, puts it upside down on his head, then takes the wire-netting under one arm and the tool-box under the other. He turns to the kitchen door, his head lost inside the cradle*)

(*The hall door opens slowly.*

THE HONOURABLE ROBIN STEBBINGTON *peers round the door. He is a young man of twenty-four, extremely well-groomed and wearing full morning attire. He carries a small parcel and a square attaché-case. He shows some surprise on seeing Henry with the cradle on his head. He cannot, of course, see Henry's face*)

ROBIN (*tentatively*) Er—excuse me——
HENRY (*stopping*) Eh?
ROBIN. —is this the—er—Hornett residence?
HENRY. The . . . ? Blimey! 'Ang on. I'll be with you in a minute. (*He is having difficulty with his load*)
ROBIN (*moving* C) Sorry to barge in like this . . .
HENRY. That's O.K.

(ROBIN *crosses to* RC *and tries unsuccessfully to peep under the cradle and see Henry's face*)

ROBIN. I rang the front-door bell, but I don't think you heard me because of the wireless.
HENRY. Wireless?
ROBIN (*trying to shake hands with Henry*) It sounded like one of those "angry old women" plays. By the way, my name is Stebbington. Robin Stebbington.
HENRY (*moving nearer the kitchen door*) Pleased to meet you.
ROBIN. Er—thanks. I—I am the P.S. to the P.S. to H.R.H.
HENRY. Ah! Then you're just the chap for the job. D'you mind?
ROBIN (*puzzled*) Not at all. What?
HENRY. Opening the D.O.O.R.
ROBIN (*puzzled*) D.O.O. . . . ? (*Brightly*) Oh, I see. (*He crosses and opens the kitchen door*) There you are, sir.
HENRY. T.A.

(HENRY *exits to the kitchen.* ROBIN *looks at the plaque on the wall* L *of the door and reacts*)

ROBIN (*calling*) I *shall* see you again?
HENRY (*off*) Yes.
ROBIN. T.A. Oh—thanks. (*He puts his case and the parcel on the table, picks up Emma's hat from the floor and puts it on the sofa then crosses to the fireplace. He sees the picture of the Queen over the mantelpiece and stands to attention for a moment. He sees an ornament on the mantelpiece, picks it up and looks at it. Not offensively, but surprised*) Good God! What is it?

(EDIE *dashes in from the hall*)

EDIE (*seeing Robin; startled and loudly*) Oh!

(*The suddenness of the entry and the "Oh!" cause* ROBIN *to drop the ornament. It breaks in two pieces*)

(*Alarmed, but distrait*) Oooh! (*She crosses to* c) You shouldn't've *done* that.

ROBIN (*alarmed and bewildered*) I—I . . . (*He stoops quickly, picks up the pieces of ornament and gapes at Edie*)

EDIE. 'Scuse me—can't stop—one or two things . . . (*She runs to the sideboard and has difficulty in opening the drawer*) Ooh! This drawer! (*She opens the drawer, takes out one or two articles which she puts on the table beside Robin's parcel. She dashes back and extracts a folded pinafore which she quickly unfolds and holds against herself*) Yes, that's mine. (*To Robin. Distrait*) Pretty, isn't it? (*She gives a little sob as she throws the pinafore loosely over the other articles and Robin's parcel on the table*) Now—anything else? (*She takes a photograph of Trevor Howard from the drawer*) Yes. Look! My "Great Sorrow". (*She shows the photograph to Robin, dashes to the drawer, searches quickly in it, slams the drawer shut, returns to the table, scoops up the articles under the pinafore, including Robin's parcel, crosses swiftly to the hall door and turns. She points to the broken ornament*) I should get rid of that before Emma sees it.

(EDIE *furtively opens the door, peeps out, then exits quickly to the hall, closing the door behind her.* ROBIN *gapes after her then looks guiltily at the broken ornament in his hands. He stands, uncertain what to do with it. At last, he crosses to* c *and puts the pieces, one by one, into the tail pocket of his morning coat.*

HENRY *enters from the kitchen*)

HENRY (*moving down* RC) Now then—here we are. (*He stops, startled by Robin's elegance*) Blimey! Are you the chap who . . . ? (*He indicates the kitchen door*)

ROBIN. Yes, rather. (*He smiles*) And you're the chap who . . . ? (*He taps his head*)

HENRY. 'S'right—Henry 'Ornett. (*He takes out his pipe*) Now, let's see. Who did you say you were?

ROBIN. Stebbington—Robin Stebbington.

HENRY. Yes, I got *that*, but the other bit. What was it? P.T.O. to the Y.M.C.A.

ROBIN (*startled*) Not exactly. Er—P.S. to the P.S. to H.R.H.

HENRY (*after a slight pause*) Oh! Interesting job?

ROBIN. Oh, I dunno. Well down the ladder.

HENRY. Ah! (*Out of his depth and puzzled*) Any overtime?

ROBIN (*blinking at him*) Are you quite sure you know what my—er—job is?

HENRY. Not absolutely quite.

ROBIN. Well, it means that I'm the P.S.—*Private* Secretary to the P.S.—*Personal* Secretary—to H.R.H.—Her Royal Highness.

HENRY (*profoundly*) Ah!

ROBIN. I'm sorry I didn't make that clear in the first place. You see, I was in a bit of a flap. I went all the way down to Portsmouth this morning.

HENRY. Did you?

ROBIN. Well, you see, we understood at the R.R. . . .

F

HENRY. Sorry—R.R.?

ROBIN. Sorry—Royal Residence.

HENRY. Sorry. O.K.

ROBIN. We understood that the christening was taking place down there.

HENRY. Christening? Ah, now I get you. (*He moves* R) It's Albert and our Shirley you want to see.

ROBIN. Able-Seaman Tufnell and his wife.

HENRY. That's right. (*He moves* RC) Albert and our Shirley.

ROBIN. Quite. Well, I motored down to Portsmouth, but their next-door neighbour told me the christening was taking place here. So, of course, I had to scoot up here and . . .

HENRY (*moving to* R *of Robin*) I hope they give you petrol money.

ROBIN (*bewildered*) Well—not exactly . . .

HENRY (*nudging Robin; encouragingly*) But you manage to fiddle it.

ROBIN (*pressing on*) You see, I have been instructed to pick up the gift of a christening mug and deliver it personally to—er—Albert and your Shirley—on behalf of—er—H.R.H.

HENRY. My goodness—you aren't half a busy lot at the R.R. We're just the same at the H.H.

ROBIN. The H.H.?

HENRY. 'Ornetts 'Ome. (*He steps back and looks at Robin*) But you needn't put your best suit on just to bring a mug down to our Shirley.

ROBIN (*pulling himself together*) Well—actually—I had to attend a wedding at St Margaret's this morning.

HENRY. H'mm! A wedding and a christening—you just want a funeral then you can about call it a day. (*Suddenly*) Here, I'm forgetting my etti-ketti. I 'aven't asked you to park yourself. (*He indicates the chair* R *of the table*) Take a pew. (*He crosses to the fireplace*)

ROBIN. Er—thanks awfully. (*He sinks on to the chair, but rises quickly with a stifled gasp of pain as he sits on the broken ornament in his tail pocket*)

(HENRY *turns and sits in the easy chair*)

(*He smiles feebly, his hand on his posterior*) I'd rather stand, if you don't mind. Been sitting a long time.

HENRY. You do just whatever you want to.

ROBIN. Thanks awfully.

(ROBIN, *during Henry's next speech, moves to* L *of the table and crosses above it to the sideboard. Keeping one eye on Henry, he extracts the broken ornament from his pocket and looks desperately around for somewhere to put it. He tries the drawers of the sideboard but they stick, and he struggles with them*)

HENRY. Couldn't believe it when I heard Shirley's kiddie was going to get a royal present. It's never 'appened before in our family—and his photograph in the paper, too, he 'ad. Grand looking kid. Hope he grows up like me. I'm a peaceful sort of chap; can't stand noise . ..

 (ROBIN *gives a good tug at the drawer and in doing so, drops a piece of the ornament with a crash*)

(*Startled*) What was that? (*He peers round the chair*)

 (ROBIN *swiftly puts the piece of ornament in his hand behind his back and stands in front of the piece on the floor*)

ROBIN. What was that?
HENRY. Sounded like something gone for a Burton.
ROBIN (*picking up the pieces*) Just what I was going to say.
HENRY (*facing front; grunting*) Edie up to her tricks. You haven't met our Edie.
ROBIN. Your Edie?
HENRY. That's a treat you can do without.

 (ROBIN, *after looking desperately around, moves to the table and drops the pieces noisily into his case*)

(*Without turning*) Coo, she is 'aving a field day.

 (EMMA *enters from the hall.* ROBIN *moves quickly below the table*)

EMMA (*as she enters*) Henry, have you . . . ?
HENRY (*rising; promptly*) Yes.

 (EMMA *sees Robin*)

EMMA (*to Henry; accusingly*) *Now* what have you brought in?

 (ROBIN *reacts*)

HENRY (*moving* RC) Emma, this is the—er—P.S. to the P.S. to . . . I forget the rest.
EMMA (*accusingly*) He 'asn't sold you anything, has he?

 (ROBIN *reacts*)

HENRY (*embarrassed*) Emma, before you lose your foot alto-gether . . . (*He beckons to her*)

 (EMMA *crosses to* L *of Henry.* ROBIN *moves* C. HENRY *grabs Emma and whispers urgently in her ear.* ROBIN *shows acute discomfort as* EMMA's *eyes rest on him*)

EMMA (*after listening to Henry for a moment*) From *where?* (*She gives Robin a hard stare*)

 (HENRY *whispers*)

He's *what?* (*She looks at Robin*)

 (HENRY *whispers*)

(*She looks disbelievingly at Robin*) Who—*him?*
F*

(ROBIN *looks uncomfortable*)

How do you *know?* Has he shown you his credits?
    HENRY. We 'adn't reached that stage.

(EMMA *looks at* ROBIN *who moves to* L *of her*)

Well—I dunno. I suppose it's all right.
    ROBIN (*tapping his waistcoat pocket*) I—I haven't a card—but I have a letter addressed to me at the R.R.—if you would care to . . . ?
    EMMA. I don't want to see no letters. If I can't take a man's word, then . . . (*She holds out her hand. Sharply*) Where is it?

(ROBIN *takes an envelope from his breast pocket and hands it to Emma*)

(*She reads the envelope*) "The Honourable Robin Stebbington." (*She stops and gapes at Robin*) Oh, my . . . ! (*She turns quickly to Henry*) Henry! (*With awe*) Henry—him—he's—Honourable!
    HENRY. So he ought to be at his age.
    EMMA (*sharply*) Henry! Where are your manners? I'll thank you to introduce me. (*She returns the envelope to Robin*) You must forgive my husband. He doesn't know what's what.
    HENRY (*introducing*) My wife—Mr—er . . .
    EMMA (*sharply*) The Honourable.
    ROBIN (*babbling*) Oh, I say—it doesn't really . . .
    EMMA (*firmly*) It *does* matter. It's a pity if we can't give the devil his due. I'm Mrs Hornett. (*She takes Robin's hand and tries to curtsy*)
    ROBIN (*dazed*) How do you . . . ?
    EMMA (*indicating Henry*) And this is my husband.
    ROBIN. Yes. I—I—rather gathered . . .

(HENRY *sits in the easy chair*)

EMMA (*overlapping*) You must excuse him if he seems a bit out of his depth, but he isn't used to moving in—social circles. (*She circles Robin, looking him up and down admiringly*) You'll know Lady Patchem, of course?
    ROBIN (*blinking*) Lady . . . ? No, I'm afraid not.
    EMMA. H'm—funny. I should've thought you would've. *She's* ever so high up, too. She opened our new Bingo Hall last week.

(ROBIN *blinks at her*)

Well, now—'aving got over the familiarities, broken the ice, as you might say—won't you sit down? (*She indicates the sofa then moves to the chair* R *of the table*)
    ROBIN (*moving to the sofa; feeling rather limp*) Thanks awfully. (*He is about to sit*)
    HENRY. The Honourable says he'd rather stand.

(ROBIN *comes to an upright position.* EMMA, *also about to sit, straightens up*)

Emma. Oh! Well, in that case, Henry . . . (*She moves to* L *of the easy chair, indicates the standing Robin, and levers Henry to his feet*)

(*There is a slight pause with all three standing rather awkwardly*)

Now—to what do we owe this intrusion?

Robin (*desperately*) Er—I've been instructed to—to . . . (*Babbling*) I say—please—wouldn't you rather sit down? I mean, there's no need for us all to stand.

(Henry *promptly sits in the easy chair*)

Emma (*gratefully*) Well, if you're sure it's all the same to you. To tell you the truth, my feet are well nigh killing me. (*She sits* R *of the table*)

(Robin *sits on the sofa*)

(*To Henry. Sharply*) Henry! It's my feet well nigh killing me, not yours.

(Henry *rises*)

Robin (*rising; babbling*) Oh, but—if Mr Hornett would like to . . .

Emma (*politely*) It's for you to say. Henry—sit!

(Henry *sits.* Robin *starts to sit*)

Oh, but *you* don't 'ave to sit because of us.

(Robin, *wretched, straightens up*)

(*She looks around*) Now we're all 'appy. (*To Robin*) You were saying?

Robin (*moving down* L *of the table*) Well, actually, it's your daughter and her husband I want to see.

Emma. What for?

Henry. He's brought the christening mug from the Princess for their kiddie.

Emma. Henry—the Honourable has a tongue in his head; let him use it. That's his job—to talk diplomatic—(*to Robin*) isn't it?

Robin (*weakly*) If I *could* see your daughter and her husband.

Emma (*to Henry*) Fetch Shirley and that husband of hers.

Henry (*rising and moving up* R) Where are they?

Emma (*sharply*) I'll tell you where they're *not*. They're not out with your ferrets.

(Henry *crosses to* c)

Tell 'em there's an Honourable to see them, and they're to act according. (*She rises, crosses to the fireplace, looks in the mirror and touches up her hair*)

(Henry *bows to Robin and exits to the hall.* Robin *grins.* Emma *turns and the grin quickly leaves* Robin's *face*)

Robin (*hastily*) This must be a proud day for you, Mrs Hornett.

EMMA (*resuming her seat* R *of the table*) No, it isn't. (*Shortly*) Far from it.

ROBIN (*moving to* L *of Emma*) But—the christening?

EMMA. I couldn't go to that christening, not if you paid me.

ROBIN. Oh, but . . .

EMMA. I've been trod on—trod on by a sailor.

ROBIN (*almost brightly*) Oh, then, of *course* you can't go. No *wonder* you wanted to sit down.

EMMA (*pointedly*) My son-in-law's defied me.

ROBIN (*realizing*) Oh!

EMMA. And what's more, he's put my daughter up to doing the same. I've been plotted against.

ROBIN. How distressing.

EMMA. You didn't think that sort of thing went on among ordinary people, did you? With royalty, of course, you 'ave it, or there'd be no 'istory. But—(*with a quick, conspiratorial look towards the hall door*) never mind that. (*She rises and crosses to* L *of Robin*) This mug . . .

ROBIN. Ah, yes, the mug.

EMMA. When those two come down, I'm going to take no interest in it. (*Quickly and sharply*) So let me see it now.

ROBIN. Oh, but that's impossible.

EMMA (*impatiently*) If I don't look at it *now*, 'ow can I keep my eyes off it *later?*

ROBIN. Now, Mrs Hornett, you wouldn't ask me to make a diplomatic *faux pas*, would you?

EMMA (*simply*) Yes. (*She pauses*) Where is it?

ROBIN (*crossing to* L *of Emma; politely but firmly*) I'm sorry, Mrs Hornett. I can't possibly show it to you first. (*Suavely*) As I had to deal with the matter personally, I can describe the mug to you.

EMMA. If I can't see it, I don't want to hear about it. (*She pauses*) What's it like?

ROBIN. Silver.

EMMA. Plate?

ROBIN. As solid as you are. (*Quickly*) Sterling silver. Most handsome—a charming, simple inscription.

EMMA (*sharply*) What's been inscripted? Not that I want to know. (*She pauses. Sharply*) Well?

ROBIN. First—the child's name—"Albert Tufnell"—then . . .

EMMA. *Albert* Tufnell?

ROBIN (*blinking*) Of course—Albert Tufnell.

EMMA (*stepping back* RC; *blazing*) You've put "*Albert* Tufnell" on that thing?

ROBIN (*baffled*) But I understood from the P.S. that . . . (*In sudden and complete panic*) Oh! Don't tell me it should have been "*Alberta*"?

EMMA (*advancing on Robin*) You!

(ROBIN *backs to the sofa*)

So you're in it, too.

Robin (*horrified*) I am—up to the neck, if . . . Mrs Hornett, please assure me I haven't made a mistake.

Emma. You never made a bigger.

Robin (*sitting on the right arm of the sofa; without diplomacy*) Blind O'Reilly! What shall I tell them when I get back to the R.R.—Royal Residence?

Emma. You can tell them Emma Hornett's finished with 'em.

Robin (*rising*) What?

Emma. Finished with the lot of 'em—and that includes you, and *you know who!* (*She moves* R)

(Robin *moves* RC)

I'm not sparing anybody's feelings, no matter how royal they might be.

Robin (*nonplussed*) But it's staggering! I could have sworn the P.S. told me Her Royal Highness said it was a boy.

Emma (*irritably*) What are you talking about? Of course it's a boy.

Robin (*gasping with relief*) It *is?* Oh! (*He sits* R *of the table*) Thank God for that! (*He wipes his brow*) Oh, you *did* give me a turn. I saw the Bloody Tower right in front of my eyes.

(Emma *starts to expostulate*)

(*Quickly*) But, Mrs Hornett, if the little b . . . (*Calmer*) If the child *is* a boy, then—er—what would appear to be the trouble?

Emma (*advancing on him*) That child was named by my son-in-law, *and* you, *and* Her Royal Highness, without me being consulted.

Robin (*babbling*) But Her Royal Highness had nothing to do with . . .

Emma. Her Royal Highness sent that mug, didn't she?

Robin. Yes, of course, but . . .

Emma. And *you* 'ad it inscripted "Albert"—you said so yourself.

Robin. Quite, but . . .

Emma (*firmly*) Then you're both accessories after the fact—the pair of you.

Robin. Mrs Hornett, I'm so sorry . . .

Emma (*moving* R; *quieter, but grumbling*) Don't say any more. I'm finished with you, my fine-feathered friend.

Robin (*rising*) Mrs Hornett . . .

Emma. If I 'ad any power in high places, I'd have you—mentioned in despatches.

Robin. But, Mrs Hornett—"Albert"—an excellent name.

Emma (*snorting*) Is it?

Robin. My father is called Albert.

Emma. *That's* no recommendation.

Robin. And, surely—the child's father is Albert, also?

Emma. And that's still less. The thought of my grandchild being named after *him* . . .

Robin. Ah! Er—quite.

(Robin *looks at Emma for a moment, then moves* c, *deep in thought. He turns, looks speculatively at her, then braces himself and crosses to* l *of her. Throughout the following scene, he becomes more and more impassioned as he presses his "argument" on Emma.* Emma *finds herself swept along by* Robin's *"oratory", and the scene should work up to a big climax*)

(*Quietly but urgently*) Mrs Hornett.

Emma (*still in high dudgeon*) Well?

Robin. You are a woman.

Emma (*blinking*) What? Well, yes—in a manner of speaking.

Robin. An Englishwoman.

Emma. 'Course I am.

Robin. An Englishwoman, and proud of being so.

Emma (*baffled*) And why not?

Robin (*agreeing*) Why not, indeed. (*He strides* c *and turns*) An Englishwoman, proud of being so—(*he strides to her*) and proud of her country.

Emma (*defiantly*) Yes.

Robin (*building up*) Proud of its history—its noble history.

Emma. Yes. (*Quickly*) Mind, I've forgotten most of it, but . . .

Robin (*sweeping on*) Proud of its tradition——

Emma (*beginning to be carried away*) Yes!

Robin. —of its monarchy.

Emma (*facing front*) Yes. (*She looks at him*) Even if I am a bit narked with you-know-who.

Robin. But . . .

Emma. But we'll forget that for the present.

Robin. Spoken like an Englishwoman. (*Quickly*) Now, Mrs Hornett. (*He moves the chair* r *of the table to* rc)

Emma (*excitedly*) Yes. (*She sits on the chair*)

Robin. You—an Englishwoman—would want to see your grandson brought up an English*man*.

Emma. Well—I 'aven't much choice—seeing he was born in Portsmouth.

Robin (*sweeping on*) But here—(*he backs and hits his chest*) here, in your big, English heart—you want him to grow up proud of his country—as you yourself have done.

Emma. He'll hear the rough side of my tongue if he doesn't.

Robin. And yet—(*he crosses to* c) and yet—Mrs Hornett, you would deny him that which is the birthright of any child, be he high or low; rich or poor.

Emma. I don't know what you mean.

Robin (*moving* c; *topping her*) I mean a *name*, Mrs Hornett. A name to be proud of. An English name.

Emma. But . . .

Robin (*crossing to* r *of her*) A name recalling doughty deeds, and gallant acts; of heroism and patriotism, Mrs Hornett.

EMMA. Yes, but . . .

ROBIN (*kneeling* R *of her*) A name that conjures up a vista of winding lanes and tranquil paths—of sylvan glades and golden corn—of white cliffs gleaming in the sun—of larks high above in the cloudless blue of an English sky.

EMMA. You mean . . . ?

ROBIN (*rising*) I mean the name—the epic name of "*Albert*", Mrs Hornett. And *that* is what you would deny your grandchild. (*He crosses above her to* C)

EMMA (*wildly*) But listen . . .

ROBIN (*crossing below the sofa to* L) A name that would stamp him for ever, and before all men as—made in England.

EMMA (*excitedly, but reluctant*) You want him called after his father?

ROBIN (*striding and thundering*) No, *no!* (*He strides wildly on and across the sofa*) A thousand times *no!*

EMMA (*bewildered*) But you just said . . .

ROBIN (*moving to* L *of Emma*) *Not* Albert after his *father*, Mrs Hornett——

EMMA. Oh!

ROBIN. —but after the untold number of English Alberts that have gone before him.

EMMA. Oh, I see.

ROBIN (*crossing above Emma to* R *of her*) Brave Alberts—golden Alberts—(*he strides up* C) royal Alberts—kings and princes.

EMMA. Well, of course . . .

ROBIN (*striding over the sofa*) Alberts who have left their names on the scrolls of fame throughout the years. *And,* let us not forget the *Albert Hall.*

EMMA (*wildly*) I went there once.

ROBIN. The Victoria and Albert Museum.

EMMA. Yes.

ROBIN (*moving to* L *of Emma*) And can we *possibly* forget the *Albert Memorial?*

EMMA (*carried away; almost jumping with excitement*) No—we can't!

ROBIN (*sweeping on*) Alberts! Alberts all! (*With great intensity*) Give him this illustrious name and his gratitude will ring in your ears for ever.

EMMA (*in agony; wildly*) Oh!

ROBIN (*crossing to* R *of Emma and hugging her*) Listen to him, Mrs Hornett! Listen to your grandson across the years. (*He declaims*) "Who gave you this name?" (*He thunders the reply*) "My Grannie! Because I am an *Englishman!*"

(EMMA *rises and stands up* L *of the easy chair.* ROBIN *stands up* R *of it*)

EMMA (*wildly; brokenly*) I'll do it! *I'll do it!*

(*They shake hands*)

ROBIN (*more wildly*) *Mrs* Hornett!
EMMA. But not because his father's called Albert.
ROBIN. Of course you're not.
EMMA. I'm doing it for England.
ROBIN. For England! (*He faces front and sings*)
                    "Rule Brit-tan-nia,

EMMA ⎱
ROBIN ⎰ (*singing together*)

                    Britannia rules the waves . . ."

(EDIE, HENRY, ALBERT *and* SHIRLEY *enter from the hall.* EDIE *carries her case and stands behind the sofa.* HENRY *crosses to* LC. ALBERT *and* SHIRLEY *remain* L.
        DAPHNE *and* CARNOUSTIE *enter from the kitchen and stand down* R)

                    "Britons never, never, *never* shall be slaves."
HENRY. Stone the crows!
EMMA (*moving* C) Henry. I've given way. My defences are down.

(ROBIN *replaces the chair* R *of the table*)

HENRY. Well, can't you pull them up?
EMMA. I'm going to let him be called "Albert" for England.
For England and the Albert Memorial.
ROBIN (*moving to* R *of Emma*) Mrs Hornett, I was wondering if
I might . . .
EMMA. Certainly. Edie.

(EDIE *puts her case on the floor up* C *and moves to* L *of Emma*)

EDIE. Yes?
EMMA. Show him where.

(EDIE, *horrified, runs up* C.
        MRS LACK *enters from the kitchen, moves to* R *of Robin, curtsies to him, then stands* L *of the easy chair*)

ROBIN. No, Mrs Hornett. I was wondering if I might make the
presentation now.
MRS LACK. What? Who's being presented?
EMMA. Not you. (*To Robin*) Right. Get on with it.
ROBIN. Thank you. (*He moves to the table*)

(EMMA *crosses to* R *of the table*)

Now, on behalf of Her Royal Highness, I have the honour . . .
(*He looks on the table*) My God! The mug! It's gone! (*He looks around*)

(*There are reactions and exclamations from the others*)

Gone!
EMMA. It can't 'ave gone. It 'asn't been.
ROBIN. It 'as—*has*. It was here on this table.
EMMA. Not when I came in, it wasn't, or I'd 'ave seen it. Eyes
of an 'awk, 'aven't I, Henry?

HENRY. You said it. I didn't. (*He moves above the sofa*)
EMMA (*picking up Robin's case*) This is yours, isn't it?
ROBIN. Yes, but . . .
EMMA. Then it's most likely in here.

(ROBIN *grabs the case. He and* EMMA *hold on to it*)

ROBIN. No, no, it isn't.
EMMA. Open it.
ROBIN. Mrs Hornett, I can't.
EMMA. Then I can. (*She snatches the case, opens it and turns it upside down. The pieces of ornament fall out*) So that's your game! Robbery! (*She picks up a piece of the ornament and holds it up*) With violence!

(EDIE *picks up her case and moves to* L *of Emma*)

EDIE. Emma, before you have him arrested, I'll say good-bye. (*She takes Emma's hand and shakes it*) I'm going out of your life for ever. I've packed all my things.
EMMA. Yours or mine? (*She points to Edie's case*) Open that!
EDIE. But . . .
EMMA. Open it in the name of the law!

(EDIE *opens her case. The parcel with the mug falls out*)

ROBIN. That's it. (*He picks up the parcel*)
EDIE. What?
ROBIN (*frantically*) It's the bloody mug. (*He tears at the wrapping*)
EDIE (*wildly and quickly*) I must've picked it up off the table by mistake. (*She picks up her things*)
ROBIN. Never mind about that. (*He crosses to Carnoustie and Daphne, still viciously opening the parcel. Almost spitting out the words*) On behalf of Her Royal Highness, I have the honour to present . . .
EMMA (*rushing to* L *of Robin*) Not to *them!* (*She spins Robin round and pushes him towards Albert and Shirley*)
ROBIN (*as he goes; wildly*) Stone the crows!

(EMMA *follows to* R *of Robin.* HENRY *moves to* R *of Emma*)

(*He pulls himself together. Formally but quickly to Albert and Shirley*) On behalf of Her Royal Highness, I have the honour to present . . . (*He takes the mug from the box and holds it up in his right hand*)

(EMMA *immediately takes the mug and turns to Henry*)

EMMA. Oh, Henry—look! Isn't it beautiful? If I thought I'd be honoured like this, I'd have a dozen babies.
HENRY. In that case, Emma we'd better hang on to that second pram.
EMMA. Why?
HENRY. You never know. We may need it ourselves.

(*A look of incredible coyness comes over* EMMA'S *face on Henry's suggestion that he and she might need a pram in the future, and she holds out her arms to him and, for the first time, positively coos)*

EMMA (*cooing*) Henry ...

HENRY, *appalled at what he seems to have let himself in for, begins to steal away as—*

the CURTAIN *falls*

FURNITURE AND PROPERTY PLOT

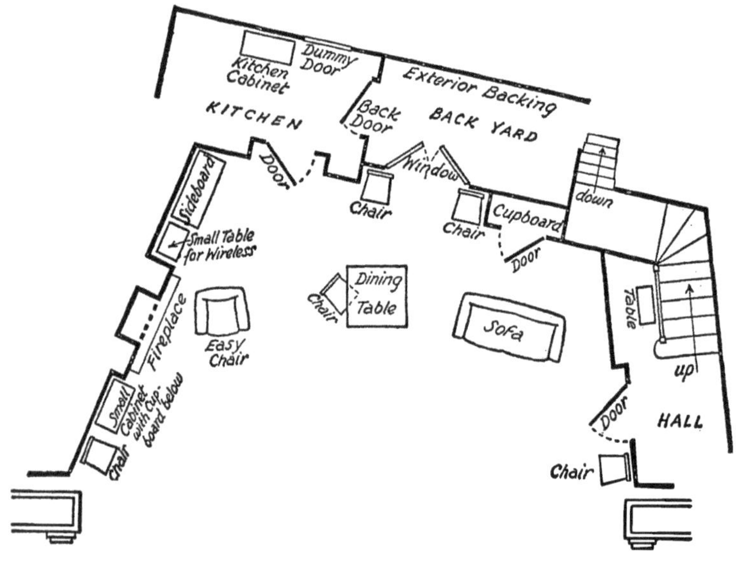

ACT I

On stage: Upright chair (down L)
> *On wall above door L:* large Victorian picture of a woman
> *On wall over cupboard door up* LC: flight of china ducks
> Sofa. *On it:* cushions, yellow chair-back
> Upright chair (L of window)
> Upright chair (R of window)
> Window curtains
> *On window-sill:* 2 ornaments
> Small dining-table. *On it:* rust chenille tablecloth
> Upright chair (R of table)
> *In cupboard over kitchen door:* vacuum cleaner tubes, boxes and paper, suitcase with old clothes, case
> *On top of cupboard:* sewing machine, boxes, rug, bird-cage
> *On back of kitchen door:* peg basket
> Sideboard. *On it:* ornaments, vase with ears of corn, photograph, 2 bottles of sauce, cruet, set of table-mats, brush and crumb tray
> *In drawer:* large white cloth
> *On wall over sideboard:* 2 brass plates

Table (above fireplace) *On it:* yellow mat, wireless, ornament,
 2 tins of tobacco, ashtray
Above fireplace: small wooden rack with letters and papers, pipe-
 rack with pipes
Fireguard
On fireplace shelves: vase with ferns, letters, ornaments, clock,
 wedding photograph, pipe, pouch with tobacco, jar with
 money in it, ashtray, mirror, comb
Fire-grate
Fire-irons
Coal scuttle
Fire-screen
On wall below fireplace: rack with letters, papers, magazines, etc.
Over mantelpiece: picture of Queen Elizabeth the Second, mirror
Easy chair. *On it:* cushion, yellow chair-back
Small cabinet (down R) *On it:* ship lamp, 2 books in book-ends
 pipe
On wall over cabinet: picture of "Bubbles"
Upright chair (down R)
Hearth rug
Rug (down RC)
Rug (below sofa)
Carpet on floor
In cupboard up LC: 2 coats, pair of plimsolls, vacuum cleaner, boxes,
 tin with medicines, etc.
In kitchen: kitchen cabinet. *On it:* bowl, mop, papers, carrier-bag
In hall: small table, pictures on wall
On floor down RC: old-fashioned wooden cradle. *In it:* pillow,
 blue pottie with bottle in it, 2 tins of Cow and Gate, 2 packets
 of Farex, large bottle of cod-liver oil
Right-hand window open
Hall door ajar
Kitchen door closed
Fire on

Off stage: Treasure cot. *In it:* golliwog (EMMA)
 Parcel (EMMA)
 Box of sausage rolls (EMMA)
 Tray. *On it:* 5 knives, 5 forks, 5 plates, 5 cups, 5 saucers, 5 tea-
  spoons (EDIE)
 Plate of bread and butter (EDIE)
 Blue carry-cot. *In it:* baby in shawl, blue cot blanket, toy (EDIE)
 Tray. *On it:* 5 large plates, plate of ham, plate of sausage rolls,
  bowl of tomatoes (EDIE)
 Teddy bear (ALBERT)
 Plate of iced cakes (EMMA)
 Photograph (SHIRLEY)
 Plate of fairy cakes (EDIE)
 Small suitcase (DAPHNE)

    Large doll (DAPHNE)
    Pink carry-cot (DAPHNE)
    Suitcase (CARNOUSTIE)
    Pillow (CARNOUSTIE)
    Rug (CARNOUSTIE)
    Baby (CARNOUSTIE)

Personal: EDIE: handkerchief
    EMMA: handkerchief, handbag. *In it:* bill
    HENRY: matches, pipe, tobacco
    ALBERT: coins
    SHIRLEY: handbag

ACT II

SCENE 1

Strike: White cloth and crockery, etc., from table
    Golliwog
    Carry-cots
    Cradle
    Parcel from sideboard
    Suitcases
    Pillow
    Blanket
    Hats and coats

Reset: Upright chairs to Act I opening positions

Set: *Down* L: cot, string, brown paper
   On table: large check cloth, brush and crumb tray
   On chair down R: Albert's cap and blouse
   On cabinet down R: Shirley's gloves
   On sideboard: headscarf
   On mantelpiece: ornament with money
Right-hand window open
All doors closed
Fire on

Off stage: Basket of groceries (EDIE)
    Blue carry-cot (ALBERT)
    Frying-pan (EDIE)
    Coat (DAPHNE)
    Cup of water (EDIE)
    Coat and umbrella (EMMA)

Personal: HENRY: pipe, tobacco, matches
ALBERT: packet of cigarettes, matches
CARNOUSTIE: tin with dog-end, matches
EDIE: handkerchief
DAPHNE: handbag. *In it:* £1 note

SCENE 2

Strike: Medicine tin, etc., from table

Set: Chair from R of table to down L of it
Blue carry-cot L of easy chair
Pink carry-cot R of chair down L of table
Babies in carry-cots, without covers
Knitting on left end of table
Right-hand window open
All doors closed
Fire on

Off stage: Bag of potatoes, open at the bottom (EDIE)
Letter (ALBERT)
Copy of *The Portsmouth Evening News* (ALBERT)
New pram (SHIRLEY)
Parcels (EMMA)
Bowl (DAPHNE)
Duster (EDIE)
New pram (HENRY)

ACT II

Strike: Prams
Carry-cots
Parcels from table
Knitting
Duster

Reset: Newspaper on cabinet down R
Chair to R of table

Set: *In sideboard drawer:* Emma's handbag, Post Office Savings book,
pinafore, photograph of Trevor Howard
Money in ornament on mantelpiece
Windows shut
All doors closed
Fire on

Off stage: Pile of underwear (EDIE)
              Coat and beret (EDIE)
              Cup of tea (EMMA)
              Cup of tea (MRS LACK)
              Roll of wire-netting (HENRY)
              Tool-box (HENRY)
              Cradle (HENRY)
              Parcel. *In it:* silver mug (ROBIN)
              Attaché-case (ROBIN)

Personal: HENRY: pipe, tobacco, matches
              ALBERT: watch
              ROBIN: envelope, handkerchief

Any character costumes or wigs needed in the performance of
this play can be hired from CHARLES H. FOX Ltd, 25 Shelton
Street, London WC2H 9HX

LIGHTING PLOT

Property fittings required: fire-grate

Interior. A living-room. The same scene throughout

THE MAIN ACTING AREAS are down R, down C, down LC, at a sofa LC
and at an easy chair RC

THE APPARENT SOURCE OF LIGHT is a window back C

ACT I. Afternoon

To open: Effect of autumn afternoon sunshine
        Fire on

No cues

ACT II, SCENE 1. Morning

To open: Effect of morning sunshine
        Fire on

No cues

ACT II, SCENE 2. Morning

To open: Lights as at the end of the previous Scene
        Fire on

No cues

ACT III. Afternoon

To open: Effect of afternoon sunshine
        Fire on

No cues

EFFECTS PLOT

ACT I

ACT III